Contents

======== ✳ ========

Dedicated to three future leaders—
Bill, Joe, and Jim

2 4 FEB 2003

THOUGHTS ON LEADERSHIP

✳

A TREASURY OF QUOTATIONS

✳

EDITED BY

WILLIAM D. HITT

BATTELLE PRESS

Columbus • Richland

Library of Congress Cataloging-in-Publication Data

Thoughts on leadership : a treasury of quotations
    by William D. Hitt

        p.   cm.
    Includes bibliographical references.
    1. Leadership—Quotations, maxims, etc.   I. Hitt, William D.
HD57 .7.T47   1991
303.3'4—dc20   91—15106
ISBN 0-935470-66-2 (hc)   CIP
ISBN 0-935470-61-1 (pbk.)

Printed in the United States of America

Copyright © 1992, Battelle Memorial Institute

All rights reserved. No part of this book may be reproduced or transmitted in any
form or by any means, electronic or mechanical, including photocopying, recording
or by any information storage and retrieval system, without permission from the
publisher.

Battelle Press
505 King Avenue
Columbus, Ohio 43201–2693
614–424–6393
1–800–451–3543
FAX: 614–424–5263

Acknowledgements

===== ✳ =====

Dr. Hitt and Battelle Press would like to thank the following individuals and organizations for permission to reprint the thoughts contained in this book. We encourage you to contact your local bookstore to expand your collections of these writers. Complete references are contained in the bibliography.

Our thanks to Warner Books, Inc.; Harcourt Brace Jovanovich, Inc.; Addison-Wesley Publishing Company; Ayesha Buber; Carol Publishing Group; Macmillan Publishing Company; John Wiley & Sons, Inc.; HarperCollins Publishers, Inc.; The University of Chicago Press; Houghton Mifflin Company; Simon & Schuster, Inc.; Penguin USA; University Associates, Inc.; Random House, Inc.; Bobbs Merrill Company; The American Management Association; William Morrow & Company, Inc.; Routledge Ltd.; Saul Gellerman; Philosophical Library of New York; Sloan School of Management; George Allen & Unwin Ltd.; Open Court Publishing Company; Schocken Books; Bantam Doubleday Dell Publishing; Yale University Press; McGraw-Hill, Inc.; The University of Pennsylvania Press; The University of California Press; Jossey-Bass, Inc.; DC Heath & Company; The Library of America; Richard D. Irwin, Inc.; Prometheus Books; Dover Publications, Inc.; Appleton-Century-Crofts; Liveright Publishing Corporation; Farrar, Straus & Giroux, Inc.; W.W. Norton & Company, Inc.; Brooks/Cole Publishing Company; L.F. Management Corporation; Harvard University Press; *Financial Executive*; Irvington Publishers, Inc.; Princeton University Press; and *Harvard Business Review*.

Foreword

— ✽ —

Dear Reader:

The development of this anthology was born out of a desire to share. Over the past 30 or so years, I have read scores of books on management and leadership. In the course of this reading, I developed a knack for extracting nuggets in the form of brief quotations. By organizing these quotations in book form, I thought that I could make a contribution to those interested in the field of leadership. My motive for undertaking this activity was to share the nuggets with others.

The book is more than a random collection of quotations. For one thing, it is *organized within a theoretical framework* that is grounded in the belief that effective leaders are, first and foremost, fully functioning persons. And secondly, it is *highly selective* in that it focuses on those ideas that can serve as principles of leadership in the present age.

The purpose of the book is to provide a set of guidelines for effective leadership — in the words of the original authors. If the book enriches your understanding of leadership and provides you with useful guidelines for action, then its purpose will have been served.

My best wishes for an enjoyable and enriching reading experience.

— Bill Hitt

The Model Leader

William D. Hitt

From the emperor down to the common people, all must regard the cultivation of the personal life as the root or foundation. There is never an orderly upshoot or superstructure when the root or foundation is disorderly.

CONFUCIOUS[1]

═══════════════ ✳ ═══════════════

LEADERSHIP JUNGLE

Large numbers of people are in search of a generic model of leadership. This includes students of leadership, practicing managers, teachers of management and leadership, and researchers. It is pretty well agreed that a generic model of leadership would provide direction for their efforts.

But is there any such thing as a generic model of leadership—one that can be adopted by many different leaders and applied in many different situations? Or is leadership so situational that it defies any effort to formulate a generic model? In other words, is the search a mere will-o'-the-wisp? This is the central question to which the paper is addressed.

A search of the relevant literature on the subject of leadership provides no definitive answer to the question. The search suggests several elements of a model—but no comprehensive model of leadership.

Looking for a generic leadership model in the literature is like trying to find your way in a jungle: the goal is clear but the way is not.

Consider the following notions about effective leadership offered by a spectrum of writers:

- Machiavelli: Effective leaders are *power-wielders,* individuals who employ cunning and subterfuge to achieve their own ends.[2]
- Max Weber: Effective leaders have *charisma*—that special spiritual power or personal quality that gives an individual influence over large numbers of people.[3]
- Frederick Taylor: Effective leaders view management as a *science.*[4]
- Max DePree: Effective leaders view management as an *art.*[5]
- Peter Drucker: Effective leaders are able to carry out the *functions of management: planning, organizing, directing, and measuring.*[6]
- Lawrence Appley: Effective leaders have mastered the art of *getting things done through others.*[7]
- Douglas McGregor: Effective leaders understand the *human side of enterprise.*[8]
- Rensis Likert: Effective leaders are able to establish effective *management systems.*[9]
- Blake and Mouton: Effective leaders choose a *leadership style* that reflects a concern for both production and people.[10]
- Hersey and Blanchard: Effective leaders choose the appropriate leadership style to *fit the situation.*[11]
- Lee Iacocca: Effective leaders focus on the three "P's": *people, productivity, and profits—in that order.*[12]

- Blanchard and Johnson: Effective leaders are able to do many of the things that they do in *one minute*.[13]
- Peters and Waterman: Effective leaders are able to do *one hundred little things well*.[14]
- Bradford and Cohen: Effective leaders *develop people*.[15]
- Peter Block: Effective leaders *empower others*.[16]
- Mark McCormack: Effective leaders learn how to apply *"street smarts"* to compensate for what they did not learn at Harvard Business School.[17]
- Rosabeth Moss Kanter: Effective leaders are *change masters*.[18]
- Bennis and Nanus: Effective leaders have *vision* and are able to translate the vision into action.[19]
- Abraham Zaleznik: Effective leaders are *twice-born*, whereas managers are only once-born.[20]
- James MacGregor Burns: Effective leaders are able to *lift followers into their better selves*.[21]

It is indeed a jungle out there! Trying to find a thread that links these many diverse notions of effective leadership is no easy task. There are too many paths and it is difficult to discern which one might lead us out of the jungle.

If we are to escape from the jungle, it is essential that we identify a *principal path*. While secondary paths may prove interesting and even enlightening, they cannot take the place of a principal path.

In his book, *On Becoming a Leader*,[22] Warren Bennis provides us with a path — or theme — for constructing a generic model of effective leadership. The focus is on the leader as a person:

> The process of becoming a leader is much the same as the process of becoming an integrated human being. For the leader, as for an integrated person, life itself is the career. Discussing the process in terms of "leaders" is merely a way of making it concrete.

THE LEADER AS A
FULLY FUNCTIONING PERSON

We now have a leitmotif, a theme, for constructing a paradigm of an effective leader. It is this idea: *the effective leader is a fully functioning person.* Granted, this is a rather general statement, and granted, we must define what we mean by "a fully functioning person." Nevertheless, it is a beginning. It may be the path that will lead us out of the jungle.

Building on the watershed postulate, we can make good use of a number of prevailing ideas in our efforts to construct a generic model of leadership. Specifically, the model will incorporate these concepts:

1. Karl Jaspers' idea of the Encompassing provides us with an outline of the fully functioning person.[23]

2. The field of humanistic psychology provides us with salient attributes of the fully functioning person.

3. James MacGregor Burns's seminal book on leadership elucidates the connection between being a fully functioning person and being an effective leader.[24]

We will stand on the shoulders of these scholars in constructing a prototype of an effective leader. This prototype is presented first in terms of "the Ladder of Self-Development." The ladder is then subdivided into specific leadership competencies. Taken as a whole, the prototype of effective leadership presented on the following pages may very well be the path that will lead us out of the jungle.

What are the attributes of an effective leader? This is the central question to which the paper is addressed. The answer proposed is in the form of a generic model of effective leadership, grounded in the idea that, first and foremost, the effective leader is a fully functioning person. This generic model then delineates 25 specific leadership competencies, capabilities essential for effective leadership. Our assumption is that any leader who possesses these 25 competencies in fair measure will be effective — not necessarily in *all* situations, but in *most* situations.

The effective leader is a fully functioning person — an integrated human being. This is the underlying premise of our description of a model leader, the cornerstone postulate supporting the entire framework.

The question then becomes: What are the attributes of a fully functioning person? No small question! A large question indeed, and one that calls for a thoughtful response.

Working from within the framework of humanistic psychology, it is possible to sketch an outline of the fully functioning person. This outline may not be definitive and highly prescriptive, but it can at least provide direction. It is then up to each person to fill in the details.

The proposed model of the fully functioning person is presented as the Ladder of Self-Development in Figure 1. The ladder consists of four rungs and two sidepieces. Each of these components represents an essential feature of the fully functioning person.

The rungs represent four modes of existence:

1. **Coping:** contending with the everyday world successfully.

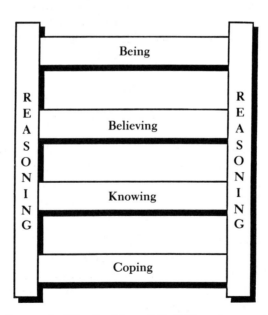

Figure 1. The Ladder of Self-Development

2. **Knowing:** comprehending facts and the truth of the objective world.
3. **Believing:** identifying with the leading ideas of movements, parties, institutions, or organizations.
4. **Being:** achieving authentic selfhood.

As indicated by the ladder, these modes of existence are arranged in a hierarchical order. The higher levels come into being only through the effects of the lower levels, but the lower levels are given direction by the higher levels. The effective leader—in his or her own self-development—continues to move up the ladder, understanding the merits of all the rungs and never getting stuck at a given rung.

The four rungs of the ladder are connected by **Reasoning.** In the words of Karl Jaspers, Reasoning is defined as "the *bond* that unites all four modes of existence. It is that through which everything else preserves its nature, is clarified, is corroborated, and is recognized. Reason is the *total will to communication.*"[25]

These are the essential components of the Ladder of Self-Development. The fully functioning person is represented by *the total ladder.* With all components intact, the leader can scale the mountain.

Given this Ladder of Self-Development as a generic paradigm of the fully functioning person, we will now examine each component of the ladder—beginning with the sidepieces.

REASONING

Manifold are the four modes of existence. What connects these four modes of existence is Reasoning.

The basic characteristic of Reasoning is the will to unity. It is Reasoning that clarifies the four modes of existence, that then prevents their isolation, and presses on toward the union of all the modes.

In paraphrasing Jaspers,[26] we can gain an appreciation of the connection between Being and Reasoning:

> The great poles of our existence are thus Being and Reasoning. They are inseparable. Being only becomes clear through Reasoning; Reasoning only has content through Being. Without Reasoning, Being is inactive, sleeping, and as though not there. Each disappears with the disappearance of the other.

Reasoning is open to all. It is not the exclusive property of professional philosophers. Reasoning is available to each person who wishes to question and to use his or her rational powers in the search for answers.

The Wheel of Reasoning presented in Figure 2 includes four spokes and a hub. These components are interconnected; together they form a unified whole.

The four spokes of the wheel represent four cognitive skills:

1. **Conceptual Skills:** the ability to deal with high order abstraction and generalization.
2. **Logical Thinking:** the ability to apply a systematic approach in solving problems.
3. **Creative Thinking:** the ability to bring into being imaginative ideas.
4. **Holistic Thinking:** the ability to grasp the total situation.

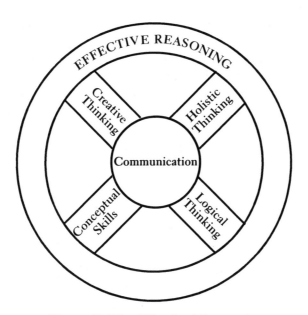

Figure 2. The Wheel of Reasoning

The four spokes of the wheel are connected by **Communication,** the *sine qua non* for Reasoning. Extrapolating from the views of Socrates and Martin Buber, we may define Communication as the interchange of thoughts, ideas, and feelings between two authentic selves in a mutual search for truth.

The leader who incorporates the Wheel of Reasoning in his or her life would be considered a philosopher in the very best sense of the term.

COPING

To cope is to contend successfully with the everyday world. Anyone working toward goals — or simply trying to survive — is confronted with obstacles along the way. How effectively these obstacles are dealt with is a measure of leadership effectiveness.

Successful coping requires power. In the parlance of everyday language, power is the ability to do or to act. It is the ability to influence others, the ability to get things done. Power is the ability to achieve the intended results.

There was a time in the history of management when the notion of power carried a negative connotation. The desire for power was limited to evil-minded persons. Today, however, we realize that power is essential to effective leadership.

The issue at hand is why a leader desires power. If a particular leader desires power only to enhance his or her own ego, or if power is viewed as an end in itself, we have reason to be cautious in our dealings with this leader. But if another leader desires power to achieve noble ends, then we have reason to befriend this leader. The central issue is motive.

Assuming that the desire for power is to achieve honorable ends, then we may construct a Wheel of Coping as shown in Figure 3. The wheel includes four spokes and a hub. Each component is an important source of influence for the leader.

These are the four spokes of the wheel:

1. **People:** a team of top-notch performers who are highly qualified and highly motivated.
2. **Information:** knowledge concerning the job, the organization, the external environment, and oneself.

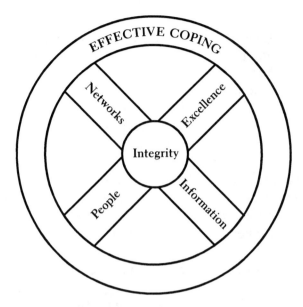

Figure 3. The Wheel of Coping

3. **Networks:** personal contacts with whom the leader can share information and resources "with the speed of a telephone call."
4. **Excellence:** striving for the highest standards in every aspect of life and achieving a reputation for always striving for the highest standards.

These four spokes are connected by the bond of **Integrity,** which is a fifth source of influence. Integrity is defined as adherence to moral principle and character. Without integrity, there is no trust; without trust, there can be no effective leadership.

The components of the wheel constitute effective sources of influence. The leader who is in possession of the entire wheel is very likely to make it to the top of the mountain.

KNOWING

Most students of leadership would agree that knowledge is power. And most also agree that, to be effective in their jobs, leaders need knowledge. But *what kind of knowledge* is needed for a leader to be effective? This is the central question.

Today, we hear much about the knowledge explosion and the accelerating rate at which knowledge is being generated. Any leader who would attempt to stay up with this knowledge explosion by storing in memory ever larger amounts of information would quickly get bogged down. And there would be no time remaining for productive work.

Effective leaders have found a solution to the problem of information overload: *they know how to identify the essential.* They have a knack for separating the wheat from the chaff. They are able to skim large amounts of information and extract the essential. They then store in memory only that which is essential—and they organize their knowledge for easy retrieval.

In a discussion that I had some years ago with a professional bridge player, I recall asking how the "real pros" were able to store such large amounts of information during the course of play. His reply was to the point: "We don't store any more information than the amateurs, but we *know* what information to store." And so it is with professional leaders.

The types of knowledge needed by the modern-day leader are shown in the Wheel of Knowing in Figure 4. Once again, the wheel includes four spokes and a hub. Each component is essential to the success of the leader.

The spokes represent four types of knowledge:

1. **Knowing the Job:** understanding the requirements of the job and how the job contributes to the organization's goals.
2. **Knowing the Organization:** understanding the culture of the organization and how to get things done effectively and efficiently.
3. **Knowing the Business One Is In:** understanding the external environment sufficiently well to judge what business you are now in and what business you should be in.

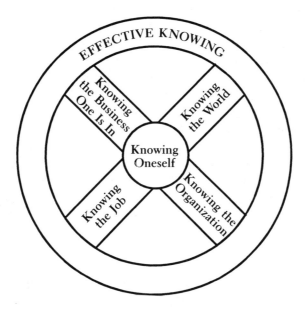

Figure 4. The Wheel of Knowing

4. **Knowing the World:** understanding the global community and how all of the smaller communities are interconnected within the larger community.

These four spokes are connected by a fifth type of knowledge: **Knowing Oneself**. As Kierkegaard aptly states: "One must know oneself before knowing anything else."[27]

With the four spokes and the hub intact, the Wheel of Knowing will contribute substantially to the leader's success.

BELIEVING

Bertrand Russell reminds us that "A way of life cannot be successful so long as it is mere intellectual conviction. It must be deeply felt, deeply believed, dominant even in dreams."[28]

And so it is with the effective leader, who has moved up the Ladder of Self-Development beyond the rung of Knowing to that of Believing. The effective leader is committed to basic beliefs that guide his or her life. As the third rung of the ladder, Believing provides direction for the lower rungs of Knowing and Coping.

The effective leader is *value-driven*. The leader's values penetrate and influence the leader's words and actions. Much of the leader's time is devoted to translating the values into action.

Importantly, the effective leader is able to elevate the values of followers. The leader does not stop with the knowledge of a follower's *present* values. This is merely the starting point. Beyond that, the leadership strategy involves elevating these values to ever higher levels. Recall Abraham Maslow's five-tiered hierarchy of human needs: physiological to safety to belongingness to self-esteem to self-actualization.[29] What the effective leader is doing is facilitating the movement of each person up the hierarchy, and as a consequence of each advancement, *new values emerge.*

The Wheel of Believing presented in Figure 5 includes four spokes and a hub. These components represent the *core functions* of leadership.

The four spokes of the wheel represent these four leadership functions:

1. **Visioning:** creating a mental picture of a desired future state of the organization.
2. **Coaching:** providing on-the-job counseling that will help followers acquire the knowledge, skills, and attitudes necessary for achieving the vision.
3. **Motivating:** helping to lift others to their higher selves in their striving to achieve the vision.
4. **Team Building:** developing a team of people who work collaboratively to achieve the vision.

The hub of the wheel represents a fifth—and a most important—leadership function: **Valuing.** In the present context, we may define Valuing as establishing one's first principles and guiding one's life by these principles. Without this function, the others are for naught.

As stated previously, the Wheel of Believing encompasses the core functions of leadership. Leaders who fully grasp the entire wheel are very likely to be effective leaders.

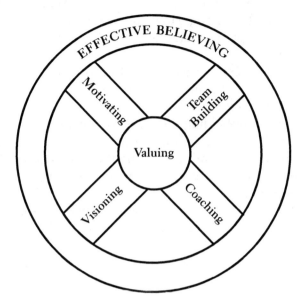

Figure 5. The Wheel of Believing

BEING

On the Ladder of Self-Development, the effective leader masters the rungs of Coping, Knowing, and Believing. But our model leader does not remain stuck at this third rung. There still remains an important step in the journey: the movement to Being.

We are now at the level of existence that constitutes authentic selfhood. At the level of Coping, the individual's identity is immersed in actions and consequences. At the level of Knowing, it is immersed in common understanding of objective knowledge. And at the level of Believing, it is immersed in the ideas and values of a particular community. But nowhere has the individual been revealed as a unique person, as an authentic self. Only at the level of Being do we find the individual revealed as a genuine person—as an authentic self.

The lower rungs of the ladder are given direction by Being. What one decides to believe is determined by Being. What one decides to know is determined by Being. How one decides to cope is determined by Being. An appropriate metaphor is that Being is the rudder that guides the ship.

It is in the advancement from the third rung of the ladder to the fourth that we uncover the principal difference between managers and leaders. Effective managers generally make it to the third rung. But being committed to upholding the values of the organizations of which they are a part, they are unwilling to transcend these values. Leaders, on the other hand, functioning as authentic selves, do not hesitate to call the organization's values into question. And this is why they are recognized as leaders.

The Wheel of Being shown in Figure 6 includes four spokes and a hub. These components represent the leader's character.

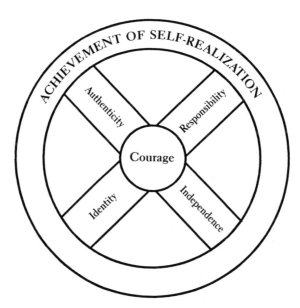

Figure 6. The Wheel of Being

The spokes represent four aspects of character:

1. **Identity:** knowing who one is and who one is not, having a sense of wholeness and integration.
2. **Independence:** being an inner-directed person rather than an other-directed person.
3. **Authenticity:** revealing one's true being to others.
4. **Responsibility:** being accountable for one's decisions and actions.

These four spokes are held in place by a fifth aspect of character: **Courage.** This essential bond that connects the others may be defined as affirming one's authentic being despite obstacles.

With all components intact, the leader will be recognized as a person of true character.

SUMMING UP

The basic thesis of this paper is that the effective leader is, first and foremost, a fully functioning person. Just as evolution serves as the integrative theory of biology, the idea of the leader as a fully functioning person can serve as the integrative theory of leadership.

By developing the basic thesis within the framework of humanistic psychology, we are able to formulate a prototype comprised of five leadership dimensions and 25 specific leadership competencies. These dimensions and competencies are listed in Figure 7. Our basic belief is that leaders who possess these competencies in fair measure will be effective in most situations.

This model is not a definitive theory of leadership, but a conceptual framework that could lead to a definitive theory. At a minimum, we have achieved "construct validity," in that we have elaborated on Burns's notion of transforming leadership. What is now needed is "empirical validity," which can be achieved only by correlating the 25 leadership competencies with measures of leadership effectiveness. But inasmuch as the conceptual model is sufficiently consistent with empirical findings on leadership effectiveness, it could be used immediately. (See especially references 30, 31, 32, and 33.)

REASONING	• Conceptual Skills • Logical Thinking • Creative Thinking • Holistic Thinking • Communication
COPING	• People • Information • Networks • Excellence • Integrity
KNOWING	• Knowing the Job • Knowing the Organization • Knowing the Business One Is In • Knowing the World • Knowing Oneself
BELIEVING	• Visioning • Coaching • Motivating • Team Building • Valuing
BEING	• Identity • Independence • Authenticity • Responsibility • Courage

Figure 7. Leadership Competencies

This generic model of leadership can shed light on the age-old question: Are leaders born or made? The question, phrased this way, is too global. It is more fruitful to focus on the 25 leadership competencies and consider the possible effect of both heredity and environment on each competency. When considering such competencies as Power through Networks, Knowing the Organization, and Communicating, most would agree that environment is the principal determinant. But when considering such competencies as Conceptual Skills, Logical Thinking, and Creative Thinking, many would argue that heredity plays an important role. Thus, it would seem that such an analytical approach would prove useful in dealing with the age-old question of nature versus nurture.

At the more practical level, there are several immediate uses of the generic leadership model:

1. Self-development of leadership competencies
2. Formal education and training of leaders
3. Selection of leaders
4. Evaluation of leaders.

In the meantime, we can hope that researchers will conduct empirical studies to further validate the model. Such empirical validity will lead to greater credibility and, in turn, greater usefulness. And that is what it is all about.

In closing, we will end with a beautiful quotation from the book, *The Leadership Challenge:*

> Wanting to lead and believing that you can lead are only the departure points on the path to leadership. Leadership is an art, a performing art. And in the art of leadership, the artist's instrument is the self. The mastery of the art of leadership comes with the mastery of the self. Ultimately, leadership development is a process of self-development.[34]

REFERENCES

1. Lin Yutang (Ed.), *The Wisdom of Confucius*, Random House (The Modern Library), 1938, p. 140.
2. Niccolò Machiavelli, *The Prince*, The New American Library, 1980.
3. H. H. Gerth and C. Wright Mills (Eds.), *From Max Weber: Essays in Sociology*, Oxford University Press, 1958.
4. Frederick Taylor, *Scientific Management*, Dartmouth College, 1912.
5. Max DePree, *Leadership is an Art*, Doubleday, 1989.
6. Peter Drucker, *Management: Tasks, Responsibilities, Practices*, Harper & Row, 1973.
7. Lawrence Appley, *Management in Action: The Art of Getting Things Done Through People*, American Management Association, 1956.
8. Douglas McGregor, *The Human Side of Enterprise*, McGraw-Hill, 1960.
9. Rensis Likert, *The Human Organization: Its Management and Value*, McGraw-Hill, 1967.
10. Robert Blake and Jane Mouton, *The New Managerial Grid*, Gulf Publishing Company, 1978.
11. Paul Hersey and Kenneth Blanchard, *Management of Organizational Behavior*, Prentice-Hall, 1977.
12. Lee Iacocca, *Iacocca: An Autobiography*, Bantam Books, 1984.
13. Kenneth Blanchard and Spencer Johnson, *The One Minute Manager*, William Morrow, 1982.
14. Thomas Peters and Robert Waterman, *In Search of Excellence: Lessons from America's Best-Run Companies*, Harper & Row, 1982.
15. David Bradford and Allan Cohen, *Managing for Excellence*, John Wiley & Sons, 1984.
16. Peter Block, *The Empowered Manager: Positive Political Skills at Work*, Jossey-Bass, 1987.
17. Mark McCormack, *What They Don't Teach You at Harvard Business School*, Bantam Books, 1984.
18. Rosabeth Moss Kanter, *The Change Masters*, Simon and Schuster, 1983.
19. Warren Bennis and Burt Nanus, *Leaders: The Strategies for Taking Charge*, Harper & Row, 1985.

20. Abraham Zaleznik, "Managers and Leaders: Are They Different?" *Harvard Business Review*, May-June 1977.
21. James MacGregor Burns, *Leadership*, Harper & Row, 1978.
22. Warren Bennis, *On Becoming a Leader*, Addison-Wesley, 1989, p. 4.
23. Karl Jaspers, *Reason and Existenz*, The Noonday Press, 1955.
24. James MacGregor Burns, *op. cit.*
25. Karl Jaspers, *op. cit.*, p. 64.
26. Karl Jaspers, *op. cit.*, pp. 67–68.
27. Robert Bretall (Ed.), *A Kierkegaard Anthology*, Random House (The Modern Library), 1946, p. 6.
28. Bertrand Russell, *New Hopes for a Changing World*, Simon and Schuster, 1951, p. 16.
29. Abraham Maslow, *Motivation and Personality*, Harper & Row, 1970.
30. Bernard Bass, *Leadership and Performance Beyond Expectations*, The Free Press, 1985.
31. Thomas Horton, *"What Works for Me": 16 CEOs Talk About Their Careers and Commitments*, Random House, 1986.
32. James Kouzes and Barry Posner, *The Leadership Challenge*, Jossey-Bass, 1987.
33. Morgan McCall, Michael Lombardo, and Ann Morrison, *The Lessons of Experience: How Successful Executives Develop on the Job*, Lexington Books, 1988.
34. James Kouzes and Barry Posner, *op. cit.*, p. 298.

Prologue

✳

A NEW LEADERSHIP MODEL

The process of becoming a leader is much the same as the process of becoming an integrated human being. For the leader, as for any integrated person, life itself is the career. Discussing the process is terms of "leaders" is merely a way of making it concrete.

WARREN BENNIS
On Becoming a Leader, p. 4

✳ ✳ ✳

THE NEED FOR A
COMPREHENSIVE VIEW OF LEADERSHIP

If there was ever a moment in history when a comprehensive strategic view of leadership was needed, not by a few leaders in high office but by large numbers of leaders in every job, from the factory floor to the executive suite, from a McDonald's fast-food franchise to a law firm, this is certainly it.

WARREN BENNIS and BURT NANUS
Leaders, p. 2

WHAT IS LEADERSHIP?

If we know all too much about our leaders, we know far too little about *leadership*. We fail to grasp the essence of leadership that is relevant to the modern age and hence we cannot agree even on the standards by which to measure, recruit, and reject it. . . . Leadership is one of the most observed and least understood phenomena on earth.

> JAMES MacGREGOR BURNS
> *Leadership*, pp. 1–2

✳ ✳ ✳

LEADERSHIP IS LIKE BEAUTY

To an extent, leadership is like beauty: it's hard to define, but you know it when you see it.

> WARREN BENNIS
> *On Becoming a Leader*, p. 1

COMMON PATTERNS OF LEADERSHIP BEHAVIOR

If we define leadership as not merely a property or activity of leaders but as a *relationship* between leaders and a multitude of followers of many types, if we see leaders as interacting with followers in a great merging of motivations and purposes of both, and if in turn we find that many of those motivations and purposes are common to vast numbers of humankind in many cultures, then could we expect to identify patterns of leadership behavior permitting plausible generalizations about the ways in which leaders generally behave?

JAMES MacGREGOR BURNS
Leadership, p. 30

✳ ✳ ✳

POWER AND LEADERSHIP

We must see power—and leadership—as not things but as *relationships*. We must analyze power in a context of human motives and physical constraints. If we can come to grips with these aspects of power, we can hope to comprehend the true nature of leadership—a venture far more intellectually daunting than the study of naked power.

JAMES MacGREGOR BURNS
Leadership, p. 11

TRANSFORMING LEADERSHIP

Transforming leadership, while more complex than transactional leadership, is more potent. The transforming leader recognizes an existing need or demand of a potential follower. But, beyond that, the transforming leader looks for potential motives in followers, seeks to satisfy higher needs, and engages the full person of the follower. . . . Woodrow Wilson called for leaders who, by boldly interpreting the nation's conscience, could lift a people out of their everyday selves. That people can be lifted *into* their better selves is the secret of transforming leadership.

JAMES MacGREGOR BURNS
Leadership, p. 4, p. 462

* * *

MANAGERS AND LEADERS

Most societies, and that includes business organizations, are caught between two conflicting needs: one, for managers to maintain the balance of operations, and one for leaders to create new approaches and imagine new areas to explore. Where managers act to limit choices, leaders work in the opposite direction, to develop fresh approaches to long-standing problems and to open issues for new options. Because managers and leaders are basically different types of people, the conditions favorable to the growth of one may be inimical to the other.

ABRAHAM ZALEZNIK
"Managers and Leaders: Are They Different?"

A CONDITION OF THE HEART

Leadership is much more an art, a belief, a condition of the heart, than a set of things to do. The visible signs of artful leadership are expressed, ultimately, in its practice.

MAX DePREE
Leadership is an Art, p. 136

✳ ✳ ✳

BEING EFFECTIVE AS A PERSON

A manager is effective in his job role only to the degree that he is effective as a *person*. . . . Managers and people who report to them are by definition interdependent: what each does affects the others. If managers focus on their own personal development as well as that of the employees reporting to them, the effects will be synergistic.

NORMAN MAIER
The Appraisal Interview, p. 206

✳ ✳ ✳

IDEALS

Ideals serve well as our guides. They are like beacons on a journey; they do not permit us to tarry, as though our goal and rest were already contained in them.

KARL JASPERS
Philosophy of Existence, p. 27

THE NEED FOR IDEALS

From Freud we learned that the past exists *now* in the person. Now we must learn, from growth theory and self-actualization theory that the future also *now* exists in the person in the form of ideals, hopes, duties, tasks, plans, goals, unrealized potentials, mission, fate, destiny, etc. One for whom no future exists is reduced to the concrete, to hopelessness, to emptiness.

ABRAHAM MASLOW
Toward a Psychology of Being, P. 214

✳ ✳ ✳

TO SEE THE POSSIBILITIES

In order to grasp the reality, we must see the *possibilities.* In the present, a formulation of the possibilities is the area in which I gain certainty concerning what I decide; without a vision of the possibilities, I act blindly; only a knowledge of the possibilities enables me to know what I am actually doing.

KARL JASPERS
Three Essays, p. 238

✳ ✳ ✳

THE SOURCE OF AIMS AND IDEALS

The aims and ideals that move us are generated by imagination. But they are not made out of imaginary stuff. They are made out of the hard stuff of the world of physical and social experience.

JOHN DEWEY
A Common Faith, p. 49

IDEAS NEED NOURISHMENT

Ideas become powerful only if they appear in the flesh; an idea which does not lead to action by the individual and by groups remains at best a paragraph or a footnote in a book—provided the idea is original and relevant. It is like a seed stored in a dry place. If the idea is to have influence, it must be put into the soil, and the soil is people and groups of people.

ERICH FROMM
The Revolution of Hope, p. 150

✳ ✳ ✳

A REPRESENTATIVE CHARACTER

A representative character is a kind of symbol. It is a way by which we can bring together in one concentrated image the way people in a given social environment organize and give meaning and direction to their lives. In fact, a representative character is more than a collection of individual traits or personalities. It is rather a public image that helps define, for a given group of people, just what kinds of personality traits it is good and legitimate to develop. A representative character provides an ideal, a point of reference and focus, that gives expression to a vision of life. . . .

ROBERT BELLAH AND ASSOCIATES
Habits of the Heart, p. 39

THOUGHTS
ON
LEADERSHIP

*

A TREASURY OF
QUOTATIONS

*

I

The Fully Functioning Person

Each human organism is conceived with a potential for becoming a complete human being—as a seed contains the potential for becoming a complete plant. But his becoming may be completed in an infinite variety of ways.

FRANCIS WILSON
"Human Nature and Aesthetic Growth"

═══════════════ ❋ ═══════════════

The Ladder of Self-Development

Reasoning

Coping

Knowing

Believing

Being

The Ladder of Self-Development

MAN IS A LADDER

Man is a ladder placed on the earth and the top of it touches heaven. And all his movements and doings and words leave traces in the upper world.

MARTIN BUBER
Ten Rungs, p. 40

* * *

A SINGLE ULTIMATE GOAL

It looks as if there were a single ultimate value for humankind, a far goal toward which all persons strive. This is called variously by different authors self-actualization, self-realization, integration, psychological health, individuation, autonomy, creativity, productivity, but they all agree that this amounts to realizing the potentialities of the person, that is to say, becoming fully human, everything that the person *can* be.

ABRAHAM MASLOW
Toward a Psychology of Being, p. 153

THE SEDUCTION

Man was — and still is — easily seduced into accepting a particular *form* of being human as his *essence*.

ERICH FROMM
The Revolution of Hope, p. 56

* * *

THE IMPORTANCE OF ALL FUNCTIONS

The truth of the matter is that all functions are important, and to center upon a position of becoming that depends upon one alone is to deliver a one-sided picture of growth in human personality.

GORDON ALLPORT
Becoming, pp. 57–58

* * *

A UNIFIED CONCEPT OF HUMANKIND

I would define a specialist as a person who no longer sees the forest of truth for the trees of fact. The challenge is how to attain, how to maintain, and how to restore a unified concept of man in the face of scattered data, facts, and findings supplied by a compartmentalized science of man.

VIKTOR FRANKL
The Will to Meaning, p. 20

THE LADDER OF SELF-DEVELOPMENT

THE UNITY OF THE HUMAN SYSTEM

Dismemberment of a comprehensive entity produces incomprehension of it and in this sense the entity is logically unspecifiable in terms of its particulars. . . . Take a watch to pieces and examine, however carefully, its separate parts in turn, and you will never come across the principles by which the watch keeps time.

> MICHAEL POLANYI
> *The Study of Man*, p. 45, p. 47

* * *

MOVING UP THE LADDER

Life must be lived on a higher plane. We must go up to a higher platform, to which we are always invited to ascend; there, the whole aspect of things changes.

> RALPH WALDO EMERSON
> "New England Reformers"
> *Essays and Lectures*, p. 601

* * *

ASCENT

No limits are set to the ascent of man, and to each and everyone the highest stands open. Here it is only your personal choice that decides.

> MARTIN BUBER
> *Ten Rungs*, p. 71

A RISING SERIES

The binding together of the modes of existence is here in the form of a rising series where the succeeding can be real only under the conditions set by the preceding. ... The higher levels are made possible by the effects of the lower and, perhaps, influenced by them. The lower on the other hand are given direction by the higher in always determinate ways.

KARL JASPERS
Reason and Existenz, pp. 88–89

* * *

POTENTIALITY

Potentiality is experienced as *mine*—my power, my question—and, therefore, whether it goes over into actuality depends to some extent on me—where I throw my weight, how much I hesitate ...

ROLLO MAY
Love and Will, p. 243

Reasoning

THE PHILOSOPHER'S IDEAL

The philosopher's ideal is that of a rational being coexisting with other rational beings. He wants to doubt, he thirsts for objections and attacks, he strives to become capable of playing his part in the dialogue of ever-deepening communication, which is the prerequisite of all truth and without which there is no truth.

KARL JASPERS
Way to Wisdom, p. 166

* * *

YEARNING FOR THE IRRATIONAL

There is something inside all of us that yearns not for reason but for mystery. ... not for penetrating clear thought but for the whisperings of the irrational... not for science but for wizardry disguised as science ... not for rationally founded influence but for magic.

KARL JASPERS
Reason and Anti-Reason in Our Time, pp. 67–68

THE MAGICIAN

The magician refuses to have his truth put to the test; he seems to be blind to the difference between truth and untruth, reality and appearance. He cannot really converse with others; he cannot engage in a candid discussion. He is biased by his ideas, both by those he forms for himself and those he takes over. He goes through life a personification of the will to power, never seeing through his own motives.

KARL JASPERS
Reason and Anti-Reason in Our Time, p. 73

❊ ❊ ❊

SEPARATION OF REASON AND REALITY

A thinker erects an immense building, a system which embraces the whole of existence and world history, etc.—and if we contemplate his personal life, we discover to our astonishment this terrible and ludicrous fact, that he himself personally does not live in this immense high-vaulted palace, but in a barn alongside of it, or in a dog kennel, or at most in the porter's lodge.

SÖREN KIERKEGAARD
The Sickness Unto Death, pp. 176–77

REASONING

SOCRATIC THINKING

(Socratic thinking) is a kind of thinking which does not permit a man to close himself. It will not put up with the evasions of those who refuse to bare their innermost thought; it shakes the complacency of those who trust blindly to fortune, who content themselves with a life of the instincts, or who become too narrowly involved in the interests of existence. This kind of thinking opens men's minds and involves the risk of openness.

KARL JASPERS
The Great Philosophers I, p. 31

* * *

THE NATURE OF REASON

Let me try to characterize Reason. Reason has no assured stability: it is constantly on the move. Once it has gained a position it presses on to criticize it and is therefore opposed to the tendency to free oneself from the necessity for all further thought by once and for all accepting irrevocably fixed ideas. It demands a careful thoughtfulness — it is therefore the opposite of mere capriciousness.

KARL JASPERS
Reason and Anti-Reason in Our Time, pp. 38–39

REASON AS A MEDIUM

I can speak of Reason, personify it, and pay my respects to it as the condition of all truth for me. But it is never a permanent thing; rather it constitutes a continuous task in time. It is not an end in itself, but rather a medium. It is that through which everything else preserves its nature, is clarified, is corroborated, and recognized. It is as though without reason everything were asleep like a seed.

KARL JASPERS
Reason and Existenz, p. 131

✳ ✳ ✳

THE MENTAL SPACE

Reason creates the mental space where everything that is can be caught, acquire language and hence validity as a being in its own right. This "space" which Reason provides is like the water, air and light in which all life can thrive and is therefore eager to be filled with such life, but on condition that it is permeated by Reason.

KARL JASPERS
Reason and Anti-Reason in Our Time, p. 58

REASONING

REASON AND REALITY

Unlike the abstract thinking of the mere intellect, rational thinking absorbs the abstractions, transcends them, and returns with them to reality. Such concrete thinking has content and visuality. It is not self-sufficient. It uses fruitful abstractions as a means of achieving clarity and a deeper penetration of reality, but it never loses its grip on what it relates to, where it comes from, whence it draws substance and significance: reality itself.

KARL JASPERS
The Future of Mankind, p. 210

* * *

REASON AND INTELLECT

Intellect is not the same as reason. Our common usage, in which we scarcely distinguish between intellectual and rational, makes it harder to put into philosophical terms what true humanity does — or can do, at least — while thinking. The intellect determines, defines, delimits, and thus clarifies things for us. Reason opens doors, provides impulses, and forbids us to rest on what we know.

KARL JASPERS
Philosophical Faith and Revelation, p. 74

THE FULLY FUNCTIONING PERSON

ON DOING YOUR OWN THINKING

But every man who philosophizes is himself and cannot simply choose the philosophy of another. He will adopt it, will convert it into a being of his own, will be awakened and illuminated by the other who speaks to him in a philosophical work—but he will maintain his testing, questioning posture.

KARL JASPERS
Philosophy II, p. 299

✳ ✳ ✳

ON SUBJECTING
ITSELF TO CRITICISM

Reason must in all its undertakings subject itself to criticism; should it limit freedom of criticism by any prohibitions, it must harm itself, drawing upon itself a damaging suspicion.

IMMANUEL KANT
Critique of Pure Reason, p. 329

✳ ✳ ✳

THE NEED FOR PRACTICE

Reason itself does not work instinctively, but requires trial, practice, and instruction in order gradually to progress from one level of insight to another.

IMMANUEL KANT
On History, p. 13

REASONING

THE CHALLENGE

The struggle of the mind to keep itself free from every sort of bondage — to remain curious, open, unsatiated in all its relations with nature — is tenfold more difficult than the cultivation of a stable, satisfying point of view, but a thousandfold more precious.

GARDNER MURPHY
Human Potentialities, p. 126

* * *

THE CONNECTING LINK

Reason as a fundamental attitude would be the connecting link between persons alien to one another, of different historical origin. It would make possible a growing communication between the developing manifoldness which knows itself held together within the Unity which belongs to no one and to which all belong.

KARL JASPERS
Reason and Anti-Reason in Our Time, p. 64

* * *

AN OPEN SECRET

Reason is like an open secret that can become known to anyone at any time; it is the quiet space into which everyone can enter through his own thought.

KARL JASPERS
Reason and Anti-Reason in Our Time, p. 92

Coping

YOUR DAILY LIFE

Your daily life is your temple and your religion.
When you enter into it take with you your all.

KAHLIL GIBRAN
The Prophet, p. 78

* * *

LIFE WASTES ITSELF

Tomorrow will be like today. Life wastes itself
while we are preparing to live. Our friends and
fellow-workers die off from us.

RALPH WALDO EMERSON
"Prudence", *Emerson's Essays*, p. 171

* * *

A RENDEZVOUS WITH LIFE

Had you forgotten that you have a rendezvous with life, here,
now, now? If you do not know how to enjoy the being and the
becoming of the present instant with all its interrelated details
and active potentialities waiting to be awakened, how can you
ever get to a being and a becoming that you will know how to
enjoy better?

JOHN RADER PLATT
The Step to Man, p. 182

COPING

ONLY ONE REALITY

We have only one reality, and that is here and now. What we miss by our evasions will never return, but if we squander ourselves, then too we lose being. Each day is precious: a moment can be everything.

KARL JASPERS
Way to Wisdom, p. 144

* * *

CONCRETE WORLD REALITY

Lived life is tested and fulfilled in the stream alone. With all deference to the world continuum of space and time I know as a living truth only concrete world reality which is constantly, in every moment, reached out to me.

MARTIN BUBER
Between Man and Man, p. 12

* * *

THE NEXT DEED

The key to truth is the next deed, and this key opens the door if one does what one has to do in such a way that the meaning of the action here finds its fulfillment. . . . Thus truth in the world of man is not to be found as the content of knowledge, but only as human existence. One does not express it, one does not perceive it, but one lives it, and receives it as life.

MARTIN BUBER
The Origin and Meaning of Hasidism, pp. 228–29

THE HEIGHTENING OF REALITY

And the reality of the experienced world is so much the more powerful the more powerfully I experience it and realize it. Reality is no fixed condition, but a quantity which can be heightened. Its magnitude is functionally dependent upon the intensity of our experiencing.

MARTIN BUBER
Pointing the Way, p. 28

* * *

THE IMPORTANCE OF EACH ACTION

Each action can be the one on which all depends; what is decisive is only the strength and concentration of hallowing with which I do it. To the question of what had been the most essential matter for his late teacher, a disciple answered, "Always just what he was engaged in at the moment."

MARTIN BUBER
The Origins and Meaning of Hasidism, p. 52

COPING

INACTION IS A KIND OF ACTION

But inaction itself is a kind of action, and it has consequences. Consistently and absolutely maintained, inaction would necessarily lead to swift ruin; it would be a form of suicide. A refusal to enter into the world is a refusal to meet the challenge of reality which darkly demands that I dare and find out what will happen. In my situation I bear the responsibility for what occurs because I do not intervene; if I can do something and don't do it, I am guilty of the consequences of my inaction.

KARL JASPERS
Philosophy II, p. 216

✳ ✳ ✳

ON RISKING

He who risks and fails can be forgiven. He who never risks and never fails is a failure in his whole being.

PAUL TILLICH
The Eternal Now, p. 144

✳ ✳ ✳

CONFRONTING THE SITUATION

One can spend a lifetime assigning blame, finding the cause "out there" for all troubles that exist. Contrast this with the "responsible attitude" of confronting the situation, bad or good, and, instead of asking "What caused the trouble? Who was to blame?" asking "How can I handle this present situation to make the most of it? What can I salvage here?"

ABRAHAM MASLOW
Abraham Maslow: A Memorial Volume, (edited by Bertha Maslow) p. 86

MEETING CONFLICTS HEAD ON

Growth in personality occurs as a consequence of meeting conflicts and impasses head on, and reconciling them. Interpersonal conflicts and impasses constitute problems which require solution so that a satisfying relationship may be maintained. Whenever a person encounters a problem in his everyday living, he is obliged to vary his behavior until he discovers some mode of responding which is successful in achieving a solution.

SIDNEY JOURARD
Healthy Personality, p. 231

* * *

ON ASSERTING ONESELF

For if one is unable to assert oneself, one is unable to participate in a genuine relationship.

ROLLO MAY
Love and Will, p. 146

* * *

AVOIDANCE OF TRUE COMMUNICATION

An avoidance of true communication is tantamount to a relinquishment of my self-being; if I withdraw from it I am betraying not only the other but myself.

KARL JASPERS
Philosophy II, p. 54

COPING

THE POSITIVE ASPECTS OF CONFLICT

But we cannot avoid *conflict*, conflict with society, other individuals and with oneself. Conflicts may be sources of defeat, lost life and a limitation of our potentiality but they may also lead to greater depth of living and the birth of more far-reaching unities, which flourish in the tensions that engender them.

KARL JASPERS
General Psychopathology, pp. 326–27

* * *

CONFLICT AS A SIGN OF HEALTH

Conflict itself is, of course, a sign of relative health as you would know if you ever met really apathetic people, really hopeless people, people who have given up hoping, striving, and coping.

ABRAHAM MASLOW
The Farther Reaches of Human Nature, p. 34

* * *

MOVING AHEAD

But one achieves selfhood only by moving ahead, despite conflict, guilt, isolation and anxiety. If one does not move ahead, the result is ultimately neurotic anxiety.

ROLLO MAY
Psychology and the Human Dilemma, p. 68

Knowing

PENETRATING THROUGH THE SURFACE

Knowing means to penetrate through the surface, in order to arrive at the roots, and hence the causes; knowing means to "see" reality in its nakedness. Knowing does not mean to be in the possession of the truth; it means to penetrate the surface and to strive critically and actively in order to approach truth ever more closely.

ERICH FROMM
To Have Or To Be? p. 40

* * *

PERSONAL KNOWLEDGE

For, as human beings, we must inevitably see the universe from a certain center lying within ourselves and speak about it in terms of a human language shaped by the exigencies of human intercourse. Any attempt rigorously to eliminate our human perspective from our picture of the world must lead to absurdity.

MICHAEL POLANYI
Personal Knowledge, p. 3

KNOWING

CONTRIBUTION OF THE PERSON KNOWING

I have shown that into every act of knowing there enters a passionate contribution of the person knowing what is known, and that this coefficient is no mere imperfection but a vital component of his knowledge.

MICHAEL POLANYI
Personal Knowledge, p. xiv

✳ ✳ ✳

COMMITMENT TO THE WHOLE

It is the act of commitment in its full structure that saves personal knowledge from being merely subjective. Intellectual commitment is a responsible decision, in submission to the compelling claims of what in good conscience I conceive to be true.

MICHAEL POLANYI
Personal Knowledge, p. 65

✳ ✳ ✳

THE MIND IS CREATING

We imagine that our mind is a mirror, that it is more or less accurately reflecting what is happening outside us. On the contrary, our mind itself is the principal element of creation. The world, while I am perceiving it, is being incessantly created for myself in time and space.

RABINDRANATH TAGORE
Personality, p. 47

THE FULLY FUNCTIONING PERSON

SEEING THE WORLD THROUGH TEMPLETS

Man looks at his world through transparent patterns or templets which he creates and then attempts to fit over the realities of which the world is composed. The fit is not always very good. Yet without such patterns the world appears to be such an undifferentiated homogeneity that man is unable to make any sense out of it. Even a poor fit is more helpful to him than nothing at all.

GEORGE KELLY
A Theory of Personality, pp. 8–9

✳ ✳ ✳

ON MAP-MAKING

Our view of reality is like a map with which to negotiate the terrain of life. If the map is true and accurate, we will generally know where we are, and if we have decided where we want to go, we will generally know how to get there. If the map is false and inaccurate, we generally will be lost.

M. SCOTT PECK
The Road Less Traveled, p. 44

KNOWING

MAP-MAKING REQUIRES EFFORT

We are not born with maps; we have to make them, and the making requires effort. The more effort we make to appreciate and perceive reality, the larger and more accurate our maps will be. But many do not want to make this effort. Their maps are small and sketchy, their views of the world narrow and misleading.

M. SCOTT PECK
The Road Less Traveled, pp. 44–45

* * *

EXPOSING OUR MAPS TO CRITICISM

A life of total dedication to the truth also means a life of willingness to be personally challenged. The only way that we can be certain that our map of reality is valid is to expose it to the criticism and challenge of other map-makers. Otherwise we live in a closed system — within a bell jar, to use Sylvia Plath's analogy, rebreathing only our own fetid air, more and more subject to delusion.

M. SCOTT PECK
The Road Less Traveled, p. 52

THE FULLY FUNCTIONING PERSON

MAPS MUST BE REVISED

But the biggest problem of map-making is not that we have to start from scratch, but that if our maps are to be accurate we have to continually revise them. ... The process of making revisions, particularly major revisions, is painful, sometimes excruciatingly painful. And herein lies the major source of many of the ills of mankind.

M. SCOTT PECK
The Road Less Traveled, p. 52

✳ ✳ ✳

DEDICATION TO TRUTH

Truth or reality is avoided when it is painful. We can revise our maps only when we have the discipline to overcome that pain. To have such discipline, we must be totally dedicated to truth. That is to say that we must always hold truth, as best we can determine it, to be more important, more vital to our self-interest, than our comfort.

M. SCOTT PECK
The Road Less Traveled, pp. 50–51

✳ ✳ ✳

WORDS OF WISDOM
Say not, "I have found *the* truth," but rather, "I have found *a* truth."

KAHLIL GIBRAN
The Prophet, p. 55

Believing

A WAY OF LIFE

A way of life cannot be successful so long as it is mere intellectual conviction. It must be deeply felt, deeply believed, dominant even in dreams.

BERTRAND RUSSELL
New Hopes for a Changing World, p. 16

* * *

ON FAITH

And Rabbi Mendel was a really believing man. He once said to himself: "I have faith; faith is clearer than vision."

MARTIN BUBER
Tales of the Hasidim (Later Masters), p. 41

* * *

FAITH ENGAGES ONE'S ENTIRE BEING

My rationality, my rational power of thought, is merely a part, a particular function of my nature; when however I "believe" . . . my entire being is engaged, the totality of my nature enters into the process, indeed this becomes possible only because the relationship of faith is a relationship of my entire being.

MARTIN BUBER
Two Types of Faith, p. 8

THE FULLY FUNCTIONING PERSON

FAITH IS ITS OWN REALITY

Faith *is*, faith creates, faith carries. It is not derived from, nor created, nor carried by anything except its own reality.

DAG HAMMARSKJÖLD
Markings, p. 142

* * *

THE NATURE OF FAITH

Faith is a call to commitment, a readiness to strive, sacrifice, stake a life on an outcome and a fulfillment. To have faith is to have a sense of values worth living for; to try to be faithful to an ideal or a vision of possibilities.

ALGERNON BLACK
"Our Quest for Faith: Is Humanism Enough?"
(in Kurtz, p. 76)

* * *

COMMITMENT

Commitment is, in paraphrase, the statement, "This I am; this I believe; this I do. I am the being, the believing, the doing." . . . Commitment is "playing for keeps" rather than vainly pleading for "slips (to) go over," as do small children in their games of marbles.

J.F.T. BUGENTAL
The Search for Authenticity, p. 338

FAITH AS ULTIMATE CONCERN

Faith as ultimate concern is an act of the total personality. It happens in the center of the personal life and includes all its elements. Faith is the most centered act of the human mind.

PAUL TILLICH
Dynamics of Faith, p. 4

✳ ✳ ✳

A SELECTED MOTIVE

Every healthy individual guides his life by a selected motive which takes precedence over all the others. He is the man who maintains his integrity in the midst of change, his individuality in the face of external pressures to conform.

HUBERT BONNER
On Being Mindful of Man, p. 171

✳ ✳ ✳

DEVOTION

By devotion I mean the aware decision to orient one's being as fully as may be possible toward the expression of some value experienced as centrally significant to one's being . . . . Devotion is a choice to focus one's being in a certain way, to bring one's faith, commitment, creativity, and love into coordination with a particular value and purpose.

J.F.T. BUGENTAL
The Search for Authenticity, pp. 355–56

PROVIDING UNITY AND DIRECTION

The ultimate concern gives depth, direction, and unity to all other concerns and, with them, to the whole personality.

PAUL TILLICH
Dynamics of Faith, p. 105

* * *

ONLY ONE ULTIMATE CONCERN

Two ultimate concerns cannot exist alongside each other. If they did, the one or the other or both would not really be ultimate.

PAUL TILLICH
Biblical Religion and the Search for Ultimate Reality,
pp. 58–59

* * *

THE TYRANNY OF PRELIMINARY CONCERNS

We maintain our preliminary concerns as if they were ultimate. And they keep us in their grasp if we try to free ourselves from them. Every concern is tyrannical and wants our whole strength. Every concern tries to become our ultimate concern, our god.

PAUL TILLICH
The New Being, pp. 157–58

FAITH AND TRUTH

Faith which refuses to face indisputable facts is but little faith. Truth is always gain, however hard it is to accommodate ourselves to it. To linger in any kind of untruth proves to be a departure from the straight way of faith.

ALBERT SCHWEITZER
Joy—*Albert Schweitzer: An Anthology*, pp. 305–06

✻ ✻ ✻

FAITH AND REASON

A faith which destroys reason destroys itself and the humanity of man. . . . Reason is the presupposition of faith, and faith is the fulfillment of reason. Faith as the state of ultimate concern is reason in ecstasy. There is no conflict between the nature of faith and the nature of reason; they are within each other.

PAUL TILLICH
Dynamics of Faith, pp. 75–77

✻ ✻ ✻

A STRONG FAITH

A strong faith begets candor in communication; it makes me ready and willing to be doubted, to test myself in my own faith, to come to myself in the free, open air where the validity of any positive faith is granted even as I fight it.

KARL JASPERS
Philosophy II, p. 381

THE FULLY FUNCTIONING PERSON

FAITH REQUIRES COURAGE

To have faith requires *courage*, the ability to take a risk, the readiness even to accept pain and disappointment.

ERICH FROMM
The Art of Loving, p. 126

* * *

SHOWING RESPECT FOR
THE FAITH OF OTHERS

It behooves both you and us to hold inviolably fast to our own true faith, that is to our deepest relationship to truth. It behooves both of us to show a religious respect for the true faith of the other. This is not what is called "tolerance," our task is not to tolerate each other's waywardness but to acknowledge the real relationship in which both stand to the truth.

MARTIN BUBER
Israel and the World, p. 40

THE OPENNESS OF THE WORLD

World is so open. For some that openness is the terrorizing lack of meaning and control which makes it a rainy freeway without lines. For others it is the openness of a fresh canvas awaiting the artist's brush, a keyboard potent with music, a vast mountain range to be explored.

J.F.T. BUGENTAL
The Search for Authenticity, pp. 347–48

* * *

UNIQUENESS OF EACH PERSON

Every person born into this world represents something new, something that never existed before, something original and unique.

MARTIN BUBER
The Way of Man, p. 16

ACTUALIZATION OF UNIQUE POTENTIALITIES

In each man there is a priceless treasure that is in no other. . . .
Every man's foremost task is the actualization of his unique, un-
precedented and never-recurring potentialities, and not the repeti-
tion of something that another, and be it even the greatest, has
already achieved.

MARTIN BUBER
Hasidism and Modern Man, p. 115, p. 140

* * *

IN ONE'S OWN WAY

Only in his own way and not in any other can the one who strives
perfect himself. He who lays hold of the rung of his companion
and lets go of his own rung, through him neither the one nor the
other will be realized.

MARTIN BUBER
The Legend of the Baal-Shem, p. 42

* * *

SELECTING ONE'S OWN MODE

There is no reason that all human existence should be constructed
on some one or small number of patterns. If a person possesses
any tolerable amount of common sense and experience, his own
mode of laying out his existence is the best, not because it is the
best in itself, but because it is his own mode.

JOHN STUART MILL
On Liberty, p. 82

BEING

FOLLOW YOURSELF

I want everyone to be the way *I strive to become*—to be himself in *his* truth. "Do not follow me; follow yourself!" is the existential challenge. Self-being awakens self-being but does not force itself on it.

KARL JASPERS
Philosophy II, p. 378

✻ ✻ ✻

FOLLOWING YOUR BLISS

The way to find out about your happiness is to keep your mind on those moments when you feel most happy, when you really are happy—not excited, not just thrilled, but deeply happy. This requires a little bit of self-analysis. What is it that makes you happy? Stay with it, no matter what people tell you. This is what I call "following your bliss."

If you follow your bliss, you put yourself on a kind of track that has been there all the while, waiting for you, and the life that you ought to be living is the one you are living. Wherever you are—if you are following your bliss, you are enjoying that refreshment, that life within you, all the time.

JOSEPH CAMPBELL
The Power of Myth, p. 155, p. 92

A NEW KIND OF FREEDOM

We are fascinated by the growth of freedom from powers outside of ourselves and are blinded to the fact of inner restraints, compulsions, and fears, which tend to undermine the meaning of the victories freedom has won against its traditional enemies. . . . We have to gain a new kind of freedom, one which enables us to realize our own individual self, to have faith in this self and in life.

ERICH FROMM
Escape from Freedom, pp. 105–06

* * *

THE ESSENCE OF FREEDOM

Freedom is man's capacity to take a hand in his own development. It is our capacity to mold ourselves.

ROLLO MAY
Man's Search for Himself, p. 160

* * *

LIVING WITH ANXIETY

Freedom requires the capacity to accept, bear and live constructively with anxiety. I refer of course to the normal anxiety all of us experience at every step in our psychological growth as well as in this upset contemporary world. To be free means to face and bear anxiety; to run away from anxiety means automatically to surrender one's freedom.

ROLLO MAY
Psychology and the Human Dilemma, pp. 179–80

BEING

CO-CREATORS

And though it is arrogance to say we are the "masters of our fate," we are saved from the need to be the victims of it. We are indeed *co-creators of our fate.*

ROLLO MAY
Love and Will, p. 270

* * *

THE LOCUS OF DIRECTION

Another trend which is evident in this process of becoming a person relates to the source or locus of choices and decisions, or evaluative judgments. The individual increasingly comes to feel that this locus of evaluation lies within himself. Less and less does he look to others for approval or disapproval; for standards to live by; for decisions and choice.

CARL ROGERS
On Becoming a Person, p. 119

* * *

HONESTY AND IDENTITY

Honesty characterizes the person and enables him to create an identity, to communicate a real presence, and to establish authentic bonds with others. The individual increasingly comes to know who he is through the stand he takes when he expresses his ideas, values, beliefs, and convictions, and through the declaration and ownership of his feelings.

CLARK MOUSTAKAS
Loneliness and Love, p. 118

THE FULLY FUNCTIONING PERSON

BEING ONE'S OWN PHILOSOPHER

Each person can be, within the limits of the human condition, his own philosopher, the creator of his own personality. When properly nurtured and lovingly guided, many individuals *could*, in the idiom of their own knowledge, experience, and value-orientation, become a cross between the poet and the philosopher.

HUBERT BONNER
On Being Mindful of Man, p. 217

* * *

HAPPINESS

Happiness is the indication that man has found the answer to the problem of human existence: the productive realization of his potentialities and thus, simultaneously, being one with the world and preserving the integrity of his self.

ERICH FROMM
Man for Himself, p. 192

II

Reasoning

When Reason speaks to you, hearken to what she says, and you shall be saved. Make good use of her utterances, and you shall be as one armed. For the Lord has given you no better guide than Reason, no stronger arm than Reason. When Reason speaks to your inmost self, you are proof against Desire. For Reason is a prudent minister, a loyal guide, and a wise counsellor.

KAHLIL GIBRAN
"The Voice of the Master," p. 54

✳

Conceptual Skills

Logical Thinking

Creative Thinking

Holistic Thinking

Communication

Conceptual Skills

MANAGEMENT OF IDEAS

The new business leaders will be those who can stretch their minds beyond the management of physical resources. They will have the capacity to conceptualize broad new philosophies of business, and translate their vision into operations. To the traditional skills of managing people, material, machines, and money, they will add a challenging new skill— management of ideas.

MELVIN ANSHEN
"The Management of Ideas"

* * *

ON INTELLIGENCE

Psychologists did not manufacture the concept of intelligence. Philosophers have pondered over it, teachers have evaluated it in their pupils, and the man on the street has assumed without question that he knows what it is.

LEONA TYLER
The Psychology of Human Differences, p. 74

REASONING

THE CAPACITY FOR CONCEPTUAL THOUGHT

The purest and most complex manifestation of man's symbolic nature is his capacity for conceptual thought; that is, for thought involving sustained and high order abstraction and generalization. Conceptual thought enables man to make himself independent of the stimulus-boundness that characterizes animal thinking.

E. MARIAN KINGET
On Being Human, p. 23

* * *

FROM THE PERCEPTUAL TO THE CONCEPTUAL

The intellectual life of man consists almost wholly in his substitution of a conceptual order for the perceptual order in which his experience originally comes.

WILLIAM JAMES
Some Problems in Philosophy, p. 49

* * *

THE INTELLECT AS PROACTIVE

The mind is not a piece of blotting paper that absorbs and retains automatically. It is rather a living organism that has to search for its food, that selects and rejects according to its present conditions and needs, and that retains only what it digests and transmutes into part of the energy of its own being.

JOHN DEWEY
How We Think, pp. 261–62

CONCEPTUAL SKILLS

THE SCULPTOR

The mind, in short, works on the data it receives very much as the sculptor works on his block of stone.

WILLIAM JAMES
The Principles of Psychology I, p. 288

* * *

THE FACULTY OF JUDGMENT

It seems to us that in intelligence there is a fundamental faculty, the alteration or the lack of which, is of utmost importance for practical life. This faculty is judgment, otherwise called good sense, practical sense, initiative, the faculty of adapting one's self to circumstances.

ALFRED BINET and THEOPHILE SIMON
"New Methods for the Diagnosis of
the Intellectual Level of Subnormals"
(in Jenkins and Paterson, pp. 90–96)

* * *

ACHIEVING CLARITY

The function of reflective thought is, therefore, to transform a situation in which there is experienced obscurity, doubt, conflict, disturbance of some sort, into a situation that is clear, coherent, settled, harmonious.

JOHN DEWEY
How We Think, pp. 100–01

REASONING

BEING A GOOD JUDGE

To be a good judge is to have a sense of the relative indicative
or signifying values of the various features of the perplexing situation; to know what to let go as of no account; what to eliminate
as irrelevant; what to retain as conducive to the outcome; what
to emphasize as a clue to the difficulty.

JOHN DEWEY
How We Think, p. 123

* * *

THE IMPORTANCE OF
CONCEPTUAL STRATEGIES

There is, perhaps, one universal truth about all
forms of human cognition: the ability to deal
with knowledge is hugely exceeded by the potential knowledge contained in the environment. To cope with this diversity, man's
perception, his memory, and his thought processes early become governed by strategies for
protecting his limited capacities from the confusion of overloading.

JEROME BRUNER
On Knowing, p. 65

CONCEPTUAL SKILLS

THE KEY TO RETRIEVAL OF INFORMATION

The principal problem of human memory is not storage but retrieval. In spite of the biological unlikeliness of it, we seem to be able to store a huge quantity of information—perhaps not a full tape recording, though at times it seems we even do that, but a great sufficiency of impressions. We may infer this from the fact that recognition, the ability to recall with maximum promptings, is so extraordinarily good in human beings and that spontaneous recall, with no promptings, is so extraordinarily bad. The key to retrieval is organization or, in even simpler terms, knowing where to find information that has been put into memory.

JEROME BRUNER
On Knowing, pp. 94–95

* * *

A SELF-GENERATED COGNITIVE PROCESS

One can cite a myriad of findings to indicate that any organization of information that reduces the aggregate complexity of material by imbedding it into a cognitive process a person has constructed for himself will make that material more accessible for retrieval. We may say that the process of memory, looked at from the retrieval side, is also a process of problem solving: how can material be "placed" in memory so that it can be obtained on demand?

JEROME BRUNER
On Knowing, pp. 95–96

REASONING

UNDERSTANDING THE RELATEDNESS OF KNOWLEDGE

In content, positive knowledge is increasing at a rate that is alarming when considered in terms of what one person can know in a lifetime. But fortunately, as the bulk of knowledge increases, the organizing structures that support it also grow. So that if there is ever more knowledge, it may indeed be the case that it is ever more related: the only possible way in which individual knowledge can keep proportional pace with the surge of available knowledge is through a grasp of the relatedness of knowledge.

JEROME BRUNER
On Knowing, p. 108

* * *

FILLING OUR MEMORY WITH GOLD

The binding fact of mental life is that there is a limited capacity for processing information—our span, as it is called, can comprise six or seven unrelated items simultaneously. Go beyond that and there is overload, confusion, forgetting. As George Miller has put it, the principle of economy is to fill our seven mental-input slots with gold rather than dross. The degree to which material to be learned is put into structures by the learner will determine whether he is working with gold or dross.

JEROME BRUNER
On Knowing, p. 123

CONCEPTUAL SKILLS

TO THINK LIKE PHILOSOPHERS

Skill in generating and manipulating ideas is precisely the skill of the great philosophers — the ability to universalize from here and now to everywhere and always. If it is true that executives in the years ahead are going to be tested above all by their ability to manage ideas, then they are going to have to understand what it means to think like philosophers and develop skill in doing it.

MELVIN ANSHEN
"The Management of Ideas"

Logical Thinking

PROBLEM SOLVING AND HUMAN NATURE

Most people throughout history have spent their lives desperately trying to solve problems they did not seek out, and failure to solve those problems has all too often meant trouble and tragedy. It is hardly surprising that humankind has come to think of happiness as the absence of problems. . . . Total absence of problems would be the beginning of death for a society or an individual. We aren't constructed to live in that kind of world. We are problem-solvers by nature — problem-seekers, problem-requirers.

JOHN GARDNER
No Easy Victories, pp. 31–32

✳ ✳ ✳

WHAT IS A PROBLEM?

What is a problem? Essentially is it not a state of disorder? Suppose the ocean is cutting into the bluff on which your summer cottage stands. That area of your life occupied by the ownership of the cottage is unsettled. To bring it back to an equilibrium, to a state of order, you must make a decision and take action. Can you hold back the sea somehow? No. Can you move the house? Yes. Can you do anything else? Yes. You might sell the house. What will happen if you do nothing? You will lose the house.

EDWARD HODNETT
The Art of Problem Solving, pp. 3–4

LOGICAL THINKING

A DEFINITION

A problem exists when a person's activity has a goal but no clear or well-learned route to the goal. He has to explore and find a route. When he has found a route, he has achieved a solution though not necessarily the best solution.

ROBERT WOODWORTH
and HAROLD SCHLOSBERG
Experimental Psychology, p. 814

✳ ✳ ✳

A SYSTEMATIC APPROACH

What you might take over from the scientist — and what the scientist might apply to problems outside his specialty — is the habit of approaching problems in an organized way. Problem solving is not merely the search for order. It is the establishment and cultivation of order once it is discovered.

EDWARD HODNETT
The Art of Problem Solving, p. 5

REASONING

PICKING THE RIGHT PROBLEMS

Picking the right problems to work on may seem like a simple question, which is probably why so many managers skip lightly over a series of problems and tackle those that at first glance appear to be the worst. However, the task is not that simple. It involves several actions and the handling of much information. To pick the right problem, a manager has to know what standards of performance he is following and what is actually going on in his department; he has to recognize when a problem exists and identify clearly the problems he wants to correct; and then he has to choose the most important problems to work on first.

CHARLES KEPNER and BENJAMIN TREGOE
The Rational Manager, p. 57

* * *

SPECIFYING THE PROBLEM

It is true, as the saying goes, that a problem clearly stated is already half solved. It is also true that a problem cannot be efficiently solved unless it is precisely described. The logic of this cannot be refuted. How can you correct a problem if you don't know exactly what that problem is? No matter how urgent it may be, it will not be correctly solved without a very exact statement of what it is, and what its critical dimensions are. This pinning down the problem is what we mean by specifying the problem.

CHARLES KEPNER and BENJAMIN TREGOE
The Rational Manager, p. 73

LOGICAL THINKING

STATING THE PROBLEM

To diagnose a problem, you have first to put it into words or other symbols that define that problem exactly. Sometimes you will arrive at this statement quickly and easily. Sometimes you will find the hardest part of the problem is stating it. Then you know you have not yet identified it. Many business conferences go on for hours before the participants agree on exactly what problems are at the heart of their discussion. United Nations conferences on agenda—mere lists of problems for later discussion—may take weeks. The statement of a problem is essential to correct diagnosis.

EDWARD HODNETT
The Art of Problem Solving, p. 18

* * *

IDENTIFICATION

Distinguishing between the problem situation and the problem itself is only the first of your efforts at identification. You face two other tasks. You have to identify the *real* problem, and you have to identify the *total* problem. Doubtless more than once you have complemented yourself on your admirable efforts to solve a problem—only to discover that it is not the problem you should have solved or that it is merely part of a larger unsolved problem.

EDWARD HODNETT
The Art of Problem Solving, p. 12

SEEING THE TOTAL PROBLEM

Keeping always before you a sense of the relatedness of the parts to the whole problem is an act of synthesis. Whether you function as a chief executive or someone far down the line, your job is always to make your efforts contribute to the solution of the problem as a whole. Failure to grasp the total problem makes an executive worthless. Failure on the part of a subordinate can mean that a well-intentioned person works to solve individual problems without contributing to the solution of the whole problem—he or she may even be pulling in the wrong direction.

EDWARD HODNETT
The Art of Problem Solving, pp. 16–17

✳ ✳ ✳

IDENTIFYING THE CAUSE

Failures in problem solving trace back to one basic fact: a problem cannot be solved unless its cause is known. A problem is an unwanted effect, something to be corrected or removed. It was brought about by some specific event, or combination of events. To get rid of the effects efficiently, you must know how it came to be. Any decision based on a false cause is going to be ineffective, wastefully expensive, and sometimes downright dangerous.

CHARLES KEPNER and BENJAMIN TREGOE
The Rational Manager, p. 17

ANALYSIS

Any problem is easier to diagnose after it has been broken down into parts. .... Analysis is the foe of vagueness and ambiguity, those arch conspirators against sensible problem solving. The analytical mind insists on definiteness and completeness. One of the ways to keep a problem before you as you work on it is to boil it down to its essentials. By going over a problem enough times, you can so dominate it that you can see it as a simple structure. Perhaps you shake it down to three short questions. Perhaps you draw it in a rough diagram. Perhaps you reduce it to an algebraic equation. Perhaps you put it in a few sentences that your wife (or husband) can understand at breakfast.

EDWARD HODNETT
The Art of Problem Solving, pp. 25–26

✳ ✳ ✳

ALTERNATIVES

The more choices you have, the better your solution to a problem is likely is be. As you start your attack on a problem, therefore, you keep asking, not merely, "Is there another alternative?" You ask, "How many more alternatives are there?" The difference between the fair problem solver and the first-rate one shows up here.

EDWARD HODNETT
The Art of Problem Solving, p. 64

REASONING

SEPARATING IDEA-GETTING
AND IDEA-EVALUATION

The idea-getting process should be separated from the idea-evaluation process because the latter inhibits the former. Idea evaluation involves the testing and the comparison of solutions in the light of what is known, their probability for succeeding, and other practical considerations. It is the practical side of problem solving and is the phase of problem solving when judgment is passed on solutions. Idea getting requires a willingness to break away from past experience. It is this process that requires an escape from the bonds of learning and demands that we search for unusual approaches and entertain new and untried ideas.

NORMAN MAIER
Problem-Solving Discussions and Conferences, p. 247

* * *

CONSEQUENCES

Consideration of consequences, secondary as well as direct, is a big part of problem solving. Setting up criteria to test results is an inseparable part of your job. Sometimes your success is easily demonstrated. Sometimes, as in science, it can be demonstrated only by elaborate technical proof. Sometimes, as in art and human relations, it can be judged by opinion only. Yet you have not thought out your attack on a problem until you have estimated what the consequences of each effort to solve it will be.

EDWARD HODNETT
The Art of Problem Solving, p. 78

LOGICAL THINKING

IMPROVING YOUR PROFICIENCY IN SOLVING PROBLEMS

You can increase your skill in growing dahlias, playing poker, and investing money. If you can improve in these activities and a host of others, you can increase your proficiency in solving problems. As you sharpen your wits in dealing with the different aspects of problem solving, you respond with eagerness to the challenge of a new problem. Through patience and practice you will master the moves in what is one of the most fascinating games and one of the most useful arts.

EDWARD HODNETT
The Art of Problem Solving, p. 7

* * *

LIKE LEARNING TO PLAY BASEBALL

Learning to solve problems is like learning to play baseball. You learn to throw, to catch, to bat, to run bases, to make plays, and to execute all sorts of refinements of these basic skills. You do not learn to play baseball. You learn these basic skills separately, and you put them together in new combinations every game. So I repeat: There is no one-two-three method for solving problems. You learn the skills, and you combine them to play the game as circumstances dictate.

EDWARD HODNETT
The Art of Problem Solving, p. 194

REASONING

INVOLVING OTHERS

In problems the solutions to which involve the reactions of others, their *participation* in the problem-solving process is the best protection against unexpected responses. Where we fail to obtain such participation because we perceive the others as being in conflict with us, we virtually assure continuation of the conflict if it exists. A failure to consult others who have a stake in our decisions is often seen as an act of aggression, because it often is. An invitation to participation in decision making is an act of conciliation, a demonstration of care and concern.

RUSSELL ACKOFF
The Art of Problem Solving, p. 44

* * *

NO EASY VICTORIES

Life never was a series of easy victories (not even a series of hard victories). We can't win every round or arrive at a neat solution to every problem. But driving, creative effort to solve problems is the breath of life, for a civilization or an individual.

JOHN GARDNER
No Easy Victories, p. 30

THE BETRAYAL

If you do not express your own original ideas, if you do not listen to your own being, you will have betrayed yourself. Also you will have betrayed our community in failing to make your contribution to the whole.

ROLLO MAY
The Courage to Create, p. 3

* * *

POTENTIAL FOR CREATIVITY

Mankind is not divided into two categories, those who are creative and those who are not. There are degrees of the attribute. It is the rare individual who has it in his power to achieve the highest reaches of creativity. But many could achieve fairly impressive levels of creativity under favorable circumstances. And quite a high proportion of the population could show *some* creativity *some* of the time in *some* aspect of their lives.

JOHN GARDNER
Self-Renewal, p. 33

REASONING

THE CREATIVE PERSON

The creative person, in all realms of life, is like a child, who dares to inquire beyond the limits of conventional answers.

PAUL TILLICH
The Shaking of the Foundations, p. iii

* * *

BRINGING INTO BEING

Creativity must be seen in the work of the scientist as well as in that of the artist, in the thinker as well as in the aesthetician; and one must not rule out the extent to which it is present in captains of modern technology as well as in a mother's normal relationship with her child. Creativity, as *Webster's* rightly indicates, is basically the process of *making*, of bringing into being.

ROLLO MAY
The Courage to Create, p. 38

* * *

AN ENCOUNTER

The first thing we notice in a creative act is that it is an *encounter*. Artists encounter the landscape they propose to paint—they look at it, observe it from this angle and that. They are, as we say, absorbed in it. ... Or scientists confront their experiment, their laboratory task, in a similar situation or encounter.

ROLLO MAY
The Courage to Create, p. 39

CREATIVE THINKING

ENGAGEMENT

The encounter (in the creative act) may or may not involve voluntary effort—that is, "will power." A healthy child's play, for example, also has the essential features of encounter, and we know it is one of the important prototypes of adult creativity. The essential point is not the presence or absence of voluntary effort, but the degree of absorption, the degree of intensity; there must be a specific quality of *engagement*.

ROLLO MAY
The Courage to Create, p. 40

❊ ❊ ❊

TALENT AND CREATIVITY

The concept of encounter enables us to make clearer the important distinction between *talent* and *creativity*. Talent may well have its neurological correlates and can be studied as "given" to a person. A man or woman may have talent whether he or she uses it or not; talent can probably be measured in the person as such. But creativity can be seen only in the act. If we were purists, we would not speak of a "creative person," but only of *a creative act*.

ROLLO MAY
The Courage to Create, pp. 42–43

REASONING

COMMITMENT
TO THE ENCOUNTER

We cannot *will* to have insights. We cannot *will* creativity. But we can *will* to give ourselves to the encounter with intensity of dedication and commitment. The deeper aspects of awareness are activated to the extent that the person is committed to the encounter.

ROLLO MAY
The Courage to Create, p. 46

✳ ✳ ✳

ECSTASY

The important and profound aspect of the Dionysian principle is that of *ecstasy*. It was in connection with Dionysian revels that Greek drama was developed, a magnificent summit of creativity which achieved a union of *form and passion* with *order and vitality*. Ecstasy is the technical term for the process in which this union occurs.

ROLLO MAY
The Courage to Create, pp. 48–49

ANXIETY AND GRATIFICATION

The breakthrough (in creativity) carries with it also an element of anxiety. ... At such time I find myself having to seek a new foundation, the existence of which I as yet don't know. ... But beyond anxiety, the main feeling that comes with the breakthrough is one of gratification. We have seen something new. We have the joy of participating in what the physicists and other natural scientists call an experience of "elegance."

ROLLO MAY
The Courage to Create, pp. 63–64

* * *

COMPLETING THE GESTALT

The idea, the new form which suddenly becomes present, *came in order to complete an incomplete Gestalt with which I was struggling in conscious awareness.* One can quite accurately speak of this incomplete Gestalt, this unfinished pattern, this unformed form, as constituting the "call" that was answered by the unconscious.

ROLLO MAY
The Courage to Create, p. 66

REASONING

WHEN THE INSIGHT COMES

The insight comes at a moment of transition between work and relaxation. It comes at a break in periods of voluntary effort. . . . It is as though intense application to the problem—thinking about it, struggling with it—starts and keeps the work process going; but some part of the pattern that is different from what I am trying to work out is struggling to be born.

ROLLO MAY
The Courage to Create, p. 66

✳ ✳ ✳

THE CONSTRUCTIVE USE OF SOLITUDE

I propose that in our day this alternation of the market place and mountain requires the capacity for the *constructive use of solitude.* It requires that we be able to retire from a world that is "too much with us," that we be able to be quiet, that we let the solitude work for us and in us.

ROLLO MAY
The Courage to Create, pp. 71–72

✳ ✳ ✳

CREATIVITY AND SOLITUDE

There may be some among you who long to become creative in some realm of life. But you cannot become or remain creative without solitude. One hour of conscious solitude will enrich your creativity far more than hours of trying to learn the creative process.

PAUL TILLICH
The Eternal Now, p. 23

CREATIVE THINKING

LIMITS AS A SOURCE OF CREATIVITY

Heraclitus said, "Conflict is both king of all and father of all." He was referring to the theme I am here stating: conflict presupposes limits, and the struggle with limits is actually the source of creative productions. The limits are as necessary as those provided by the banks of a river, without which the water would be dispersed on the earth and there would be no river—that is, the river is constituted by the tension between the flowing water and the banks.

ROLLO MAY
The Courage to Create, p. 137

* * *

IMAGINATION

Imagination is the outreaching of mind. It is the individual's capacity to accept the bombardment of the conscious mind with ideas, impulses, images, and every other sort of psychic phenomena welling up from the preconscious. It is the capacity to "dream dreams and see visions," to consider diverse possibilities, and to endure the tension involved in holding these possibilities before one's attention. Imagination is casting off mooring ropes, taking one's chances that there will be new mooring posts in the vastness ahead.

ROLLO MAY
The Courage to Create, p. 144

Holistic Thinking

GRASPING THE TOTAL SITUATION

Let us look further at the essentials of leadership. Of the greatest importance is the ability to grasp a total situation. The chief mistake in thinking of leadership as resting wholly on personality lies probably in the fact that the executive leader is not a leader of men only but of something we are learning to call the total situation. This includes facts, present and potential, aims and purposes, and people. Out of a welter of facts, experience, desires, aims, the leader must find the unifying thread. He must see a whole, not a mere kaleidoscope of pieces. He must see the relation between all the different factors in a situation.

MARY PARKER FOLLETT
Freedom and Coordination, p. 51

* * *

ONE-CHANNELED MINDS

One-channeled minds can never comprehend that truth may have many channels.

GORDON ALLPORT
Becoming, p. 85

HOLISTIC THINKING

THE UNCRITICAL MIND

The uncritical mind suffers from an ineradicable tendency to look for a truth that can be recognized as universally valid and taken for the definitive whole, by which I shall know what is good, what I should do, and what reality itself is.

KARL JASPERS
Three Essays, p. 241

* * *

NO MONOPOLY OF TRUTH

No individual or group can claim a monopoly of truth. . . . We must not block the path to inquiry or research. Let us always leave open the possibility that we may be mistaken and that there may be other points of view that share in meaning and truth.

PAUL KURTZ
The Fullness of Life, p. 127

* * *

ON TRUTH

Truth is our element of life, yet if a man fasten his attention on a single aspect of truth, and apply himself to that alone for a long time, the truth becomes distorted and not itself, but falsehood; herein resembling the air, which is our natural element, and the breath of our nostrils, but if a stream of the same be directed on the body for a time, it causes cold, fever, and even death.

RALPH WALDO EMERSON
"Intellect", *Emerson's Essays*, p. 239

AN IRRATIONAL RULE

A rule of thinking which would absolutely prevent me from acknowledging certain kinds of truth if those kinds of truth were really there, would be an irrational rule.

WILLIAM JAMES
*The Will to Believe and Other Essays
on Popular Philosophy*, p. 28

* * *

THE TOTALITY OF HUMAN LIFE

Truth does not exist in thought for itself or in knowledge for itself. Truth is only the totality of human life and of the human essence.

LUDWIG FEUERBACH
Principles of the Philosophy of the Future, p. 71

* * *

AN UNCOMPROMISING ATTITUDE
TOWARD TRUTH

Is there a truth we can possess? Can we appropriate it? There certainly is none we can pick up and put in our pockets. But the individual can have an honest and uncompromising attitude toward the truth; he can have a legitimate relationship to truth and hold and uphold it all his life.

MARTIN BUBER
Israel and the World, p. 46

HOLISTIC THINKING

ACHIEVING UNITY OF THOUGHT

To be unanimous with ourselves means to preserve our thinking by relating the separate, the
contradictory, the diffuse, to a unity.

KARL JASPERS
Way to Wisdom, p. 173

* * *

VERTICAL KNOWLEDGE

By knowledge we do not merely increase the range of our information, but we can rise by steps in the way of thinking itself. If
this succeeds, we do not merely add to the endless information
about things, but, by our ability to engage in a new type of thinking, increase our insight into the whole, and gain thereby a new
consciousness of being. From the higher level it is possible to see
through the lower one, but not vice versa.

KARL JASPERS
"Reply to My Critics" (in Schilpp, p. 795)

* * *

THE TASK OF PHILOSOPHIZING

The task of philosophizing is to show facts and possibilities in
the broadest scope, to say what is and can be, and to set up yardsticks for testing what does and what does not seem consistent,
appropriate, and true.

KARL JASPERS
The Future of Mankind, p. 260

REASONING

THE MEANING OF PHILOSOPHY

The Greek word for philosopher (*philosophos*) connotes a distinction from *sophos*. It signifies the lover of wisdom (knowledge) as distinguished from him who considers himself wise in the possession of knowledge.

KARL JASPERS
Way to Wisdom, p. 12

* * *

TO CLARIFY A WHOLE

Philosophizing is a striving to clarify a whole which in the beginning is obscure. Hence it must differentiate, think the parts successively, and in this movement build up the whole.

KARL JASPERS
The Great Philosophers I, p. 318

HOLISTIC THINKING

LIVING FOR THE TRUTH

Whoever philosophizes wants to live for the truth. He questions wherever he goes, whatever he experiences, whatever men he meets, and above all he questions what he himself is thinking, feeling, doing. ... He would rather founder on truth than be happy in illusion.

KARL JASPERS
Philosophy is for Everyman, p. 119

* * *

THE PHILOSOPHICAL LIFE

The philosophical life is not, speaking generally, a unique thing, identical for all. It is like a star-shower, a myriad of meteors, which knowing not whence they come nor whither they go, shoot through life. The individual will join in the movement, to however small an extent, through the soaring of his self-existence.

KARL JASPERS
Man in the Modern Age, p. 15

Communication

THE FUNDAMENTAL FACT OF HUMAN EXISTENCE

The fundamental fact of human existence is neither the individual as such nor the aggregate as such. Each, considered by itself, is a mighty abstraction. ... The fundamental fact of human existence is man with man. What is peculiarly characteristic of the human world is above all that something takes place between one being and another the like of which can be found nowhere in nature.

MARTIN BUBER
Between Man and Man, pp. 202–03

✳ ✳ ✳

THE PATHOLOGY OF OUR TIME

That peoples can no longer carry on authentic dialogue with one another is not only the most acute symptom of the pathology of our time, it is also that which most urgently makes a demand of us. I believe, despite all, that the peoples in this hour can enter into dialogue, into a genuine dialogue with one another.

MARTIN BUBER
Pointing the Way, p. 238

COMMUNICATION

THE PROBLEM

Increasingly, I have become painfully aware of the terribleness of most communication; of people talking but not saying what they mean; of the contradiction between the outward words and expressions and the inner meanings and messages; of people looking as if they were listening without any real connection or contact with one another.

CLARK MOUSTAKAS
Loneliness and Love, p. 130

✳ ✳ ✳

ON BEING "PRESENT"

It is an undeniable fact, though it is hard to describe in intelligible terms, that there are some people who reveal themselves as "present"—that is to say, at our disposal—when we are in pain or in need to confide in someone, while there are other people who do not give us this feeling, however great is their goodwill.

GABRIEL MARCEL
The Philosophy of Existentialism, pp. 39–40

REASONING

WHAT WAS MOST IMPORTANT

Soon after the death of Rabbi Moske, Rabbi Mendel of Kotzk asked one of his disciples: "What was most important to your teacher?" The disciple thought and then replied: "Whatever he happened to be doing at the moment."

MARTIN BUBER
Tales of the Hasidim (Later Masters), p. 173

✻ ✻ ✻

THREE KINDS OF COMMUNICATION

I know three kinds (of communication). There is genuine dialogue—no matter whether spoken or silent—where each of the participants really has in mind the other or others in their present and particular being and turns to them with the intention of establishing a living mutual relation between himself and them. There is technical dialogue, which is prompted solely by the need of objective understanding. And there is monologue disguised as dialogue, in which two or more persons, meeting in space, speak with themselves in strangely and tortuous and circuitous ways and yet imagine they have escaped the torment of being thrown back on their own resources.

MARTIN BUBER
Between Man and Man, p. 19

TRUTH IN THE INTER-HUMAN SPHERE

Whatever the significance of the term "truth" is in other spheres, in the inter-human sphere its significance is that people reveal themselves to one another as they truly are in their being. . . . Wherever this is absent, the human also is not true.

MARTIN BUBER
(in Hodes, p. 191)

* * *

EXISTENTIAL COMMUNICATION

Existential communication is not to be modeled and is not to be copied; each time it is flatly singular. It occurs between two selves which are nothing else, are not representative, and are, therefore, not interchangeable. In this communication, which is absolutely historic and unrecognizable from outside, lies the assurance of selfhood.

KARL JASPERS
Philosophy II, p. 54

* * *

A MUTUAL SEARCH FOR TRUTH

For I imagine we are not striving merely to secure victory for my suggestions or for yours; rather we ought both of us to fight in support of the truth and the whole truth.

SOCRATES
"Philebus" (in Hamilton and Cairns, p. 1090)

REASONING

HELPING TO CLARIFY

In every fruitful dialogue, each participant must help the other to clarify his thought rather than to force him to defend formulations about which he may have his doubts.

ERICH FROMM
The Revolution of Hope, p. 110

* * *

CONFIRMING THE OTHER

In a genuine dialogue each of the partners, even when he stands in opposition to the other, heeds, affirms, and confirms his opponent as an existing other.

MARTIN BUBER
Pointing the Way, p. 238

* * *

KEEPING AN OPEN MIND

The one thing which has become clearer and clearer to me in the course of my life is that keeping an open mind is of the utmost importance. The right kind of openness is the most precious human possession. . . . We need to take a firm stand, but we also need to feel that we have not thus put our feet in shackles. Wherever we stand, we should stand free and unbiased and grow aware of the world.

MARTIN BUBER
Israel and the World, p. 42

COMMUNICATION

A DEFINITION

Open-mindedness may be defined as being free from prejudice, partisanship, and such other habits as close the mind and make it unwilling to consider new problems and entertain new ideas.

JOHN DEWEY
How We Think, p. 30

* * *

DESIRE FOR KNOWLEDGE

Open-mindedness is a quality which will always exist where desire for knowledge is genuine. It only fails where other desires have become entangled with the belief that we already know the truth.

BERTRAND RUSSELL
Education and the Good Life, p. 246

* * *

THE DANGER OF DOGMATISM

People who claim to be *absolutely* convinced that their stand is the only right one are dangerous. Such conviction is the essence not only of dogmatism, but of its more destructive cousin, fanaticism. It blocks off the user from learning new truth, and it is a dead giveaway of unconscious doubt. The person then has to double his or her protests in order to quiet not only the opposition but his or her own unconscious doubts as well.

ROLLO MAY
The Courage to Create, p. 13

REASONING

AWARENESS OF OTHER OPINIONS

A good way of ridding yourself of certain kinds of dogmatism is to become aware of opinions held in social circles different from your own. . . . If you cannot travel, seek out people with whom you disagree, and read a newspaper belonging to a party that is not yours. If the people and the newspaper seem mad, perverse, and wicked, remind yourself that you seem so to them.

BERTRAND RUSSELL
Unpopular Essays, p. 104

✳ ✳ ✳

UNDERSTANDING OPPOSING VIEWS

It is important to learn not to be angry with opinions different from your own, but to set to work understanding how they come about. If, after you have understood them, they still seem false, you can then combat them more effectually than if you had continued to be merely horrified.

BERTRAND RUSSELL
The Art of Philosophizing, p. 25

ALTERING YOUR VIEWS

Suppose a person can convince me of error and bring home to me that I am mistaken in thought or act; I shall be glad to alter, for the truth is what I pursue, and no one was ever injured by the truth, whereas he is injured who continues in his own self-deception and ignorance.

MARCUS AURELIUS ANTONINUS
Meditation VI (in Knight, p. 21)

✳ ✳ ✳

A PEAK EXPERIENCE

When unity of self and other is experienced and communication reaches a heightened, personal meaning, life is being lived at a peak level. At times it seems unbelievable, almost beyond reach, but when it happens it is something of awesome beauty.

CLARK MOUSTAKAS
Loneliness and Love, p. 102

III

Coping

To strive for power for power's sake means to strive for nothing. He who seizes empty power ultimately grasps at emptiness. Will to power because one needs power to realize the truth in which one believes has a constructive strength ...

MARTIN BUBER
Pointing the Way, p. 157

———————————— ❋ ————————————

People

Information

Networks

Excellence

Integrity

IMPORTANCE OF THE HUMAN FACTOR

Many of you have long experienced in your manufacturing operations the advantages of substantial, well-contrived, and well-executed machinery. If then, due care as to the state of your inanimate machines can produce such beneficial results, what may not be expected if you devote equal attention to your vital machines, which are far more wonderfully constructed?

ROBERT OWEN
A New View of Society, p. 58

* * *

PEOPLE ARE OUR GREATEST ASSET

Managers are fond of saying, "Our greatest asset is people." They are fond of repeating the truism that the only real difference between one organization and another is the performance of people. All other resources one organization commands to exactly the same extent as does any other. And most managers know perfectly well that of all the resources, people are the least utilized and that little of the human potential of any organization is tapped and put to work.

PETER DRUCKER
Management, p. 308

COPING

THE MAIN DISTORTION: UNREALIZED POTENTIAL

I become steadily more persuaded that perhaps the greatest disparity between objective reality and managerial perceptions of it is an underestimation of the potentialities of human beings for contributions to organizational effectiveness. These potentialities are not merely for increased expenditure of effort on limited jobs (although such potentialities do exist) but for the exercise of ingenuity, creativity in problem solving, acceptance of responsibility, leadership in the relational sense, and development of knowledge, skill, and judgment. When opportunities are provided under appropriate conditions, managers are regularly astonished to discover how much more people contribute than they had believed possible.

DOUGLAS McGREGOR
The Professional Manager, p. 98

* * *

THE HUMAN ORGANIZATION

All the activities of any enterprise are initiated and determined by the persons who make up that institution. Plants, offices, computers, automated equipment, and all else that a modern firm uses are unproductive except for human effort and direction. . . . Every aspect of the firm's activities is determined by the competence, motivation, and general effectiveness of its human organization. Of all the tasks of management, managing the human component is the central and most important task, because all else depends upon how well it is done.

RENSIS LIKERT
The Human Organization, pp. 148–49

PEOPLE

HUMAN ASSET ACCOUNTING

Human asset accounting refers to activity devoted to attaching dollar estimates to the value of the firm's human organization. If able, well-trained personnel leave the firm, the human organization is worth less; if they join it, the firm's human assets are increased. If bickering, distrust, and irreconcilable conflict become greater, the human enterprise is worth less; if the capacity to use differences constructively and engage in cooperative teamwork improves, the human organization is a more valuable asset.

RENSIS LIKERT
The Human Organization, pp. 148–49

* * *

THE PEOPLE BUSINESS

What is perhaps not so generally recognized is the fact that all executives, in the final analysis, are in the business of people. While the railroad executive is in the business of running a railroad, the banker in the business of finance, the automobile man in making automobiles, and the store manager in selling merchandise, they are all in the business of people.

LAWRENCE APPLEY
Management in Action, pp. 149–50

COPING

ON THE IMPORTANCE OF PEOPLE

In the end, all business operations can be reduced to three words: people, product, and profits. People come first. Unless you've got a good team, you can't do much with the other two.

LEE IACOCCA
Iacocca, p. 167

* * *

A BELIEF IN PEOPLE

I think the key to my management style is a sincere belief in people and a sensitivity to where they are and who they are and what they're trying to accomplish, so that I can anticipate some of their needs.

JAMES BURKE
(in Horton, p. 30)

PEOPLE

INTERDEPENDENCE

The outstanding fact about relationships in the modern industrial organization is that they involve a high degree of *inter*dependence. Not only are subordinates dependent upon those above them in the organization for satisfying their needs and achieving their goals, but managers at every level are dependent upon all those below them for achieving both their own and organizational goals.

DOUGLAS McGREGOR
The Human Side of Enterprise, p. 23

* * *

PEOPLE AT WORK

People at work are not so different from people in other aspects of life. They are not entirely creatures of logic. They have feelings. They like to feel important and to have their work recognized as important. Although they are interested in the size of their pay envelopes, this is not a matter of their first concern. . . . They like to be praised rather than blamed. . . . They like to know what is expected of them and where they stand in relation to their boss's expectations. . . . They like to have some warning of the changes that may affect them. . . . They like to be listened to and have their feelings and points of view taken into account. . . . In short, employees, like most people, want to be treated as belonging to and being an integral part of some group.

FRITZ ROETHLISBERGER
"The Human Equation in Employee Productivity"

COPING

ON INDIVIDUAL DIFFERENCES

Organizations are made up of all different kinds of people; their backgrounds vary; their convictions may be as wide apart as the poles; their ambitions and motivations are individual; their drives, ideas, and thinking processes follow separate patterns. The manager has to accept these differences and use them to guide the group toward the attainment of common goals. He cannot crush them and mold them into a uniform pattern, but he can temper them, influence them, and convert the organization into a dynamic, hard-hitting unit that attains its objectives.

LAWRENCE APPLEY
Management in Action, p. 157

* * *

CHOOSING THE RIGHT PEOPLE

In these difficult business times — and with our rapidly changing technology — you have to rely more on people and less on organization. Choosing the right people is essential. If you don't have smart, professional people, you can have the best organization in the world, but it will not work.

MARISA BELLISARIO
(in Horton, p. 39)

PEOPLE

GETTING THE VERY BEST PEOPLE

Business has become much more competitive on a worldwide basis. The answer to that challenge is no different than it's ever been: you've got to get better and better, and if you don't, you will be left behind. The key is to get the very best people you can, and then provide them with an environment that encourages them to handle these challenges the way they see fit.

JAMES BURKE
(in Horton, p. 16)

* * *

EVEN BETTER THAN YOU

It has always seemed to me that the smartest thing you can do is gather around the best people you can possibly find, people who — if you can do it — are better than you. All my experience suggests this is right.

HENRY B. SCHACHT
(in Horton, p. 283)

COPING

"PEOPLE" DECISIONS

An organization that wants to build a high spirit of performance recognizes that "people" decisions—on placement and pay, on promotion, demotion, and firing—are the true "control" of an organization. They, far more than the accountant's figures and reports, model and mold behavior. For the people decision signals to every member of the organization what it is that management really wants, really values, really rewards.

PETER DRUCKER
Management, p. 460

* * *

SHOWING PERSONAL CONCERN

Through the years in dozens of management training programs, I have asked hundreds of managers this question: "In all of your working life, have you ever had a supervisor or manager sit down with you and say, 'I am really interested in how you feel about your job, and how you feel about this department and the whole company. Tell me, honestly, what are the things you feel good about and what things bother you or block you? How can I help make your situation here more satisfying and productive?'" The response by managers is fairly constant—less than 25 percent say they have experienced such an interview in their total work life.

WILLIAM DYER
*Contemporary Issues in Management
and Organization Development,* p. 74

PEOPLE

TREAT PEOPLE WITH RESPECT

Treat people as adults. Treat them as partners; treat them with dignity; treat them with respect. Treat *them* — not capital spending and automation — as the primary source of productivity gains. These are fundamental lessons from the excellent companies research. In other words, if you want productivity and the financial reward that goes with it, you must treat your workers as your most important asset.

THOMAS PETERS and ROBERT WATERMAN
In Search of Excellence, p. 238

✳ ✳ ✳

CONFIRMING ONE'S POTENTIALITY

I meet another — I accept and confirm him as he now is. But confirming a person *as he is* is only the first step, for confirmation does not mean that I take his appearance at this moment as the person I want to confirm. I must take the other person in his dynamic existence, in his specific potentiality. How can I confirm what I want most to confirm in his present being? That is the hidden, or in the present lies hidden what *can become*. His potentiality makes itself felt to me as that which I would most confirm.

MARTIN BUBER
A Believing Humanism, pp. 170–71

Information

THE NEED FOR INFORMATION

We are coming to recognize with increasing clarity that the capacity of an organization to function well depends both upon the quality of its decision-making processes and upon the adequacy and accuracy of the information used. Sound decisions require accurate information about relevant dimensions of the problem as well as correct interpretation of that information. If the information available for decision making is inaccurate or is incorrectly interpreted, the diagnostic decisions are likely to be in error and the action taken, inappropriate.

RENSIS LIKERT
The Human Organization, p. 128

* * *

THE ESSENTIAL TOOL

The manager has a specific tool: information. He does not "handle" people; he motivates, guides, organizes people to do their own work. His tool—his only tool—to do all this is the spoken or written word or the language of numbers. No matter whether the manager's job is engineering, accounting, or selling, his effectiveness depends on his ability to listen and to read, on his ability to speak and to write. He needs skill in getting his thinking across to other people as well as skill in finding out what other people are after.

PETER DRUCKER
The Practice of Management, p. 346

INFORMATION AND WISDOM

I find it helpful to think of *data* as the ore, the sum total of all the undifferentiated observations—facts—that are available to be organized by somebody at a given moment in time. *Information,* then, is the result of somebody's applying the refiner's fire to that ore, selecting and organizing what is useful to somebody. But it isn't *knowledge* until I have put some part of that semifinished product to use in my own mind. ... *Wisdom* is integrated knowledge, information made super-useful by theory, which relates bits and fields of knowledge to each other, which in turn enable me to use the knowledge to do something.

HARLAN CLEVELAND
The Knowledge Executive, pp. 22–23

* * *

TWO MISSING ELEMENTS

Two of the missing elements in most management procedures are first, that the manager hasn't been asked what information he needs to be able to do the job he has committed himself to, and second, he hasn't been asked what information he needs to be able to know how he's doing. Hence, people bitterly complain that they would like to manage themselves by objectives but they can't. Most of the time the answers to both questions could be written on the back of an envelope. There are very few answers in life that can't be written on the back of an envelope.

PETER DRUCKER
(in Dowling, p. 233)

COPING

INFORMATION OVERLOAD

Managers and workers at all company levels suffer today from information overload. Endless and often unproductive meetings, stacks of daily mail, and jangling telephones leave us bug-eyed and stupefied at the end of our day's ingestion of information. ... When the contemporary worker suffers such information overload, he or she does the natural thing and simply declines to receive anymore. ... What we now call information desperately needs to be disciplined, processed, and interpreted before it can do us much good.

ROGER D'APRIX
Communicating for Productivity, p. 14

* * *

DEALING WITH INFORMATION OVERLOAD

Most managers suffer less from lack of relevant information than from an overabundance of irrelevant information. This is not a play on words; it has significant consequences in the design of information systems. It is common knowledge that most managers suffer from information overload; therefore, providing them with additional information, even relevant information, can help little because they do not have the time required to separate the wheat from the chaff. ... For this reason an effective information system should *filter* information, eliminating the irrelevant, and condense what is relevant.

RUSSELL ACKOFF
The Art of Problem Solving, pp. 202–03

INFORMATION

THE NEED FOR CONSTRAINTS AND RESTRICTIONS

To move from an unorganized state to an organized state requires the introduction of constraints and restrictions to reduce diffuse and random communication to channels appropriate for the accomplishment of organizational objectives. ... In terms of information theory, unrestricted communication produces noise in the system. Without patterning, without pauses, without precision, there is sound but there is no music. Without structure, without spacing, without specifications, there is a Babel of tongues but there is no meaning.

DANIEL KATZ and ROBERT KAHN
The Social Psychology of Organizations, p. 430

✳ ✳ ✳

WHAT INFORMATION DO I NEED?

Managers should ask themselves: "What information do I need to do my job and where do I get it?" They should make sure that whoever has to provide that information understands the manager's needs — not only in terms of what is needed but also how it is needed.

PETER DRUCKER
Management, p. 415

COPING

ON IDENTIFYING INFORMATION NEEDS

Management chronically deplores that it "does not have enough information to go on." This criticism, more often than not, is entirely correct. Yet management often has not identified its needs, nor has it demanded that these needs be identified by subordinate staff members. To determine its information needs, management must review the types of decisions it is called upon to make, the frequency of these decisions, and the specific information that might assist in securing the ultimate success of the decisions.

ROBERT HOLMES
"Developing Better Management Information Systems"

* * *

THE REQUIREMENT FOR HARD THINKING

Executives and professional specialists have to think through what is information for them, that is, what data they need: first, to know what they are doing; then, to be able to decide what they should be doing; and finally, to appraise how well they are doing. Until this happens, the now popular Management Information Systems Departments are likely to remain cost centers rather than becoming the result centers they could be.

PETER DRUCKER
The New Realities, p. 215

INFORMATION

TWO KINDS OF INFORMATION

The way doctors diagnose an illness illustrates the process (of managerial decision making). First, he must know a great deal about the nature of human beings. This knowledge is based on extensive research which relates symptoms to causes and measurements of body conditions to the health of the organism, thereby revealing the character of the human body's normal and abnormal functioning. This knowledge gives doctors insights into how the system ought to function, so that they can know what they need to measure and how they need to interpret the measurements. The second kind of information needed by doctors to discover the patient's state of health at any particular time is that revealed by the appropriate measurements and tests made on that patient at that time.

RENSIS LIKERT
The Human Organization, p. 128

* * *

FOCUSING ON THE KEY VARIABLES

Only the most important variables which have the most marked relationships and which best summarize many other variables need be reported to each operating unit. Each manager and his department need data on only a relatively few dimensions, namely, those which are operationally most important. This would conserve time and focus attention on matters having the greatest influence on the department's performance.

RENSIS LIKERT
The Human Organization, p. 144

COPING

CRITICAL SUCCESS FACTORS

Critical success factors are the limited number of areas in which satisfactory results will ensure successful competitive performance for the individual, department, or organization. CSFs are the few key areas where "things must go right" for the business to flourish and for the manager's goals to be attained.

CHRISTINE BULLEN and JOHN ROCKART
A Primer on Critical Success Factors, p. 7

✳ ✳ ✳

THE IMPORTANCE OF CSFs

Critical success factors are the relatively small number of truly important matters on which a manager should focus his or her attention. For this reason, the term "critical success factors" is aptly chosen. They represent the few "factors" which are "critical" to the "success" of the manager concerned. There are, in every manager's life, an incredible number of things to which his or her attention can be diverted. The key to success for most managers is to focus their most limited resource (their time) on those things which really make the difference between success and failure.

CHRISTINE BULLEN and JOHN ROCKART
A Primer on Critical Success Factors, p. 12

INFORMATION

MAKING CRITICAL SUCCESS FACTORS EXPLICIT

Most managers spend considerable time and energy both on the job *and* in their leisure hours thinking about those few areas of activity which are "close to the bone." Much time is spent considering ways to improve performance in each of these areas. The value of the CSF process is to make these areas *explicit*, not merely implicit. They can be used to aid in the company's planning process, to enhance communication among the firm's management, and to aid information systems development.

CHRISTINE BULLEN and JOHN ROCKART
A Primer on Critical Success Factors, pp. 12–13

* * *

A VEHICLE FOR
IDENTIFYING INFORMATION NEEDS

The CSF procedure provides top management with a vehicle for thinking about their information needs. In far too many organizations, top management has given little time to pondering their own information needs. Rather, they have been concerned with the traditional areas of marketing, manufacturing, finance, etc. In many organizations, top management has not yet made the shift to the realization that, with today's technology, it is not only feasible, but desirable (and some would say even necessary) for them to spend time thinking through their information requirements. The CSF method is a business-based, logical, and time-sparing entrée into this new endeavor for line management.

CHRISTINE BULLEN and JOHN ROCKART
A Primer on Critical Success Factors, p. 43

QUESTIONS THAT HELP ELICIT CSFs

1. "Will you please tell me, in whatever order they come to mind, those things that you see as critical success factors in your job at this time?"

2. "Let me ask the same question concerning critical success factors in another way. In what one, two, or three areas would failure to perform well hurt you the most? In short, where would you most hate to see something go wrong?"

3. "Assume you are placed in a dark room with no access to the outside world, except for food and water, today. What would you most want to know *about the business* when you came out three months later?"

CHRISTINE BULLEN and JOHN ROCKART
A Primer on Critical Success Factors, p. 55

✳ ✳ ✳

THE NATURE OF A MANAGEMENT INFORMATION SYSTEM

A management information system, simply, is an organized method of providing each manager with all the data and only those data which he needs for decision, when he needs them, and in a form which aids his understanding and stimulates his action.

BERTRAM COLBERT
"The Management Information System"

INFORMATION

TAILORING INFORMATION

An important area for the manager of the future is to obtain the right information in the right form and at the right time. Tailoring information requires a high order of intelligence and design. Until managers increasingly realize that very little of their operation can be planned and controlled through "handbook" approaches, and until more managers recognize that they themselves must become involved in tailoring the information they require, progress will continue to be slow in this area. As long as information design is confused with the clerical work of information gathering and summarizing, managers will understandably continue to fret about the inadequacy of the data on which they are forced to act.

KOONTZ, O'DONNELL and WEIHRICH
Management, p. 818

✳ ✳ ✳

MEASURING MIS SUCCESS

The degree of user satisfaction is probably the most useful index of measuring the success or effectiveness of an information system. A mediocre system can be eminently successful when supported by user participation, while a model technical system, without such support, can be a dismal failure. Human relations has much greater impact here than is generally realized; it at least equals technical expertise in importance.

ROBERT HOLMES
"Developing Better Management Information Systems"

COPING

PERSONAL OBSERVATION

In any preoccupation with the devices of managerial control, one should never overlook the importance of control through personal observation. Budgets, charts, reports, ratios, auditors' recommendations, and other devices are essential to control. But the manager who relies wholly on these devices and sits, so to speak, in a soundproof control room reading dials and manipulating levers can hardly expect to do a thorough job of control. Managers, after all, have the task of seeing that enterprise objectives are accomplished by people, and although many scientific devices aid in making sure that people are doing that which has been planned, the problem of control is still one of measuring activities of human beings. It is amazing how much information an experienced manager can get from personal observation, even from an occasional walk through a plant or an office.

KOONTZ, O'DONNELL, and WEIHRICH
Management, pp. 759–60

✳ ✳ ✳

HIGH TECH/HIGH TOUCH

Now, at the dawn of the twenty-first century, high tech/high touch has truly come of age. Technology and our human potential are the two great challenges and adventures facing humankind today. The great lesson we must learn from the principle of high tech/high touch is a modern version of the ancient Greek ideal—*balance*.

JOHN NAISBITT
Megatrends, p. 40

Networks

NETWORKS AND INNOVATION

The innovative managers agreed that the most common roadblock
they had to overcome in their accomplishment, if they faced any
at all, was poor communication with other departments on whom
they depended for information; at the same time, more than a
quarter of them were directly aided by cooperation from departments other than their own as a critical part of their innovation.
Therefore, a communication system, depending on the kind
adopted by a given corporation, can either constrain or empower
the effort to innovate.

ROSABETH MOSS KANTER
The Change Masters, p. 160

* * *

A ROADBLOCK TO INNOVATION

Sheer height of hierarchy contributed to the virtual absence of
lateral cooperation or communication and support across areas.
Peers in other parts of the company can seem irrelevant when
the structure is segmented and the culture segmentalist. People
at middle levels are more likely to guard their turf, mend their
own fences, and concentrate on pleasing their own boss than to
assist others outside their box on the organization chart. Most
often this is passive: noncontact, noncommunication. Occasion-
ally, it takes the form of active conflict. And it shows up in
managerial accomplishments.

ROSABETH MOSS KANTER
The Change Masters, p. 79

COPING

THE FAILURE OF HIERARCHIES

The failure of hierarchies to solve society's problems forced people to talk to one another—and that was the beginning of networks. In a sense, we clustered together among the ruins of the tumbled-down pyramid to discuss what to do. We began talking to each other outside the hierarchical structure, although much of our previous communication had been channeled inside. That was the birth of the networking structure.

JOHN NAISBITT
Megatrends, p. 191

✳ ✳ ✳

THE FIRST STEP

The failure of hierarchies to solve human problems has forced people to begin talking with one another outside their organizations, and that is the first step to forming a network. Clusters of people have come together to communicate about, and attempt to address, the concerns and problems that traditional structures have failed to address.

JOHN NAISBITT
Megatrends, pp. 197–98

NETWORKS

THE INFORMAL ORGANIZATION

As everyone knows, the formal channels of communication and influence as defined by the organization chart do not constitute a complete description of what goes on. There are complex patterns of communication and influence that are generally spoken of as the *informal organization*. Because it is not one coherent system, it might be more accurate to speak of *informal groups* and *informal networks*. . . . Call them what you will, they are essential to the functioning of the system.

JOHN GARDNER
On Leadership, p. 85

* * *

THE NEED FOR INFORMAL LINKAGES

A few years ago one rarely heard *network* used as a verb, but the usage has spread because it describes an increasingly necessary function: the process of creating or maintaining a pattern of informal linkages among individuals or institutions. In a swiftly changing environment, established and formal linkages may no longer serve, or may have been disrupted. New and flexible interconnections become necessary.

JOHN GARDNER
On Leadership, p. 102

COPING

A POWERFUL TOOL
FOR SOCIAL ACTIONS

As friends, as individuals, as members of small groups or large organizations, we exchanged resources, contacts, and information with the speed of a telephone call or a jet airplane ride, with the high touch of our own voices set against the din of a world swarming with too much data and too little knowledge. Networking was a powerful tool for social actions. Those who would change the world began doing it locally, in clusters of like-minded people with a single ideological purpose.

JOHN NAISBITT
Megatrends, p. 191

✳ ✳ ✳

WHAT IS A NETWORK?

Simply stated, networks are people talking to each other, sharing ideas, information, and resources. The point is often made that networking is a verb, not a noun. The important part is not the network, the finished product, but the process of getting there—the communication that creates the linkages between people and clusters of people.

JOHN NAISBITT
Megatrends, p. 192

NETWORKS

INFORMATION AS THE EQUALIZER

The "Old Boy Network" is elitist; the new network is egalitarian. Within the networking structure, information itself is the great equalizer. Networks are not egalitarian just because every member is a peer. On the contrary, because networks are diagonal and three-dimensional, they involve *people* from every possible level. What occurs in a network is that members treat one another as peers—because what is important is the information, the great equalizer.

JOHN NAISBITT
Megatrends, p. 197

* * *

SHARING INFORMATION

One of networking's great attractions is that it is an easy way to get information. Much easier, for example, than going to a library or university or, God forbid, the government. Washington Researchers, a Washington, D. C., firm specializing in obtaining government information for corporate clients, estimates that it takes seven phone calls to get the information you want from a government agency. Experienced networkers claim they can reach anyone in the world with only six interactions. It has been my experience, however, that I can reach anyone in the United States with only two—three at the very most—exchanges.

JOHN NAISBITT
Megatrends, p. 194

CREATION OF KNOWLEDGE

Although sharing information and contacts is their main purpose, networks go beyond the mere transfer of data to the creation and exchange of knowledge. As each person in a network takes in new information, he or she synthesizes it and comes up with other, new ideas. Networks share these newly forged thoughts and ideas.

JOHN NAISBITT
Megatrends, p. 194

* * *

TOWARD GREATER EFFICIENCY

We are all buried in the overload of information being generated and transmitted all around us. With networks to help, we can select and acquire only the information we need as quickly as possible. Networks cut diagonally across the institutions that house information and put people in direct contact with the person or resource they seek.

JOHN NAISBITT
Megatrends, p. 197

NETWORKS

WHOLEPARTS

In contrast to bureaucracies, whose existence hinges on members who perform highly specialized tasks and who are totally dependent on one another, networks are composed of self-reliant and autonomous participants—people and organizations who simultaneously function as independent "wholes" and as interdependent "parts." We have coined the word *wholeparts* to describe this fundamental feature of networks.

JESSICA LIPNACK and JEFFREY STAMPS
Networking, p. 7

✳ ✳ ✳

DISTRIBUTION OF POWER AND RESPONSIBILITY

Contrasting with the bureaucratic tendency to centralize control and decision making, in networks power and responsibility are distributed. Whereas bureaucracies seek to bring people and power into the hands of a dominant authority, networks deliberately create a decentralized pattern of power with many people accountable for the work of a network. Similarly, while bureaucracies function along vertical lines, with information flowing up and orders flowing down, networks function along horizontal lines with information and ideas passing from person to person and group to group.

JESSICA LIPNACK and JEFFREY STAMPS
Networking, p. 8

COPING

ON BEING "HYDRA-HEADED"

While hierarchies are rigidly constructed with steps up a pyramid of ranks to a pinnacle that houses and exalts one revered leader or board of directors, networks have many leaders and few, if any, rungs of power. Like the Hydra, the nine-headed serpent which grew two heads each time one was cut off by Hercules, a network is *hydra-headed*, speaking with many equivalent but different voices at the same time.

JESSICA LIPNACK and JEFFREY STAMPS
Networking, p. 8

❋ ❋ ❋

FUZZINESS OF ORGANIZATION

Unlike a hierarchy, whose internal parts and external boundaries can be crisply mapped on a flow chart, a network has few clear inner divisions and has indistinct borderlines. A network makes a virtue out of its characteristic *fuzziness*, frustrating outside observers determined to figure out where a network begins and ends.

JESSICA LIPNACK and JEFFREY STAMPS
Networking, p. 8

NETWORKS

MULTIPLE ROLES

Contrasting with bureaucrats, who scrupulously define their own specialized tasks and those of each underling, networkers play multiple roles, sometimes defying definition. In communicating, which is the main business of networks, a networker may in one moment serve as a *node*—an entry point or an end recipient — and in another moment serve as a *link*—a connector between nodes and conveyors of information.

JESSICA LIPNACK and JEFFREY STAMPS
Networking, pp. 8–9

* * *

SHARED VALUES

While bureaucracies bind their members through mechanisms of reward and punishment (promotions and demotions), networks cohere through the shared values of their members. If a network could be drawn on paper, its lines of coherence would consist of the ideas that the participants agree upon, manifested in commitments to similar ideals.

JESSICA LIPNACK and JEFFREY STAMPS
Networking, p. 9

COPING

A NETWORK *STYLE* OF MANAGEMENT

What is evolving now is a network *style* of management. I am not suggesting that companies will become huge corporate networks, abandoning formal controls to allow employees to spend their time talking with each other. Instead, the new management style will be inspired by and based on networking. Its values will be rooted in informality and equality; its communication style will be lateral, diagonal, and bottom up; and its structure will be cross-disciplinary.

JOHN NAISBITT
Megatrends, p. 198

* * *

EMPOWERING OTHERS

In the network environment, rewards come by empowering others, not by climbing over them. The vertical to horizontal power shift that networks bring about will be enormously liberating for individuals. Hierarchies promote moving up and getting ahead, producing stress, tension, and anxiety. Networking empowers the individual, and people in networks tend to nurture one another.

JOHN NAISBITT
Megatrends, p. 204

Excellence

TO CREATE POCKETS OF EXCELLENCE

Our evidence is clear. Even if the company is not an exciting one, we observe *pockets of excellence*. Excellence is what you, the supervisor (or vice president), create on *your* turf. . . . It can be done and it is done. . . . Major overall corporate transformations tend to be top-down, not bottom-up. But that is no excuse for not getting on with it among your people.

TOM PETERS and NANCY AUSTIN
A Passion for Excellence, p. 322

✳ ✳ ✳

A POWERFUL WORD

I find that "excellence" is a curiously powerful word—a word about which people feel strongly and deeply. But it is a word that means different things to different people. It is a little like those ink blots that psychologists use to interpret personality. As we contemplate the word "excellence" we read into it our own aspirations, our own conception of high standards, our hopes for a better world.

JOHN GARDNER
Excellence, pp. 10–11

COPING

TWO WAYS TO EVALUATE

There is a way of measuring excellence that involves comparison between people — some are
musical geniuses and some are not; and there
is another that involves comparison between
myself at my best and myself at my worst. It
is this latter comparison which enables me to
assert that I am being true to the best that is
in me — or forces me to confess that I am not.

JOHN GARDNER
Excellence, pp. 116–17

✳ ✳ ✳

A MATTER OF EFFORT

It isn't a question of whether the individual gets
to the peak of the pyramid. We can't all get to
the peak, and that isn't the point of life anyway.
The question is whether individuals, whatever
their worldly success, have continued to learn
and grow and try.

JOHN GARDNER
Excellence, p. 126

EXCELLENCE

BEYOND INFORMATION AND SKILLS

Nor are the things we learn in maturity simple things such as acquiring information and skills. We learn not to engage in self-destructive behavior. We learn not to burn up energy in anxiety. We learn to manage our tensions if we have any, which we do. We learn that self-pity and resentment are among the most toxic of drugs, and if we got addicted we break the habit at all costs.

We learn to bear with the things we can't change. We learn that most people are neither for us nor against us; they are thinking about themselves. We learn that no matter what we do, some people aren't going to love us—a lesson that is at first troubling and then quite relaxing.

JOHN GARDNER
Excellence, p. 127

* * *

THE WILL TO AFFECT EVENTS

Creativity within an organization or society is to be found among men and women who are far removed from the fatalistic end of the scale. They have a powerful conviction that they can affect events *in some measure*. Leaders at every level must help their people keep that belief. There are all too many factors in contemporary life that diminish it.

JOHN GARDNER
Excellence, p. 148

COPING

THE SELF-FULFILLING PROPHECY

Good leaders know that if they expect a lot of their constituents, they increase the likelihood of high performance. . . . That means standards, an explicit regard for excellence. In a high-morale society, people expect a lot of one another, hold one another to high standards. And leaders play a special role in conveying such expectations. Good leaders don't ask more than their constituents can give, but they often ask—and get—more than their constituents intended to give or thought it was possible to give.

JOHN GARDNER
Excellence, pp. 148–49

* * *

A MATTER OF EXPECTATION

We are beginning to understand that the various kinds of talents that flower in any society are the kinds that are valued in the society. On a visit to Holland, my wife asked our hostess why children and adults in that country showed such an extraordinarily high incidence of language skills. "We expect it of children," the woman said simply. "We think it important." High performance takes place in a framework of expectation.

JOHN GARDNER
Excellence, p. 149

BREAKING THE BARRIER

But much of human performance is conditioned by what the performer thinks is possible for him. Leaders understand that. There was a time when people thought it was physically impossible to run a four-minute mile. When Roger Bannister ran it under four minutes, he broke the physical barrier and the mental barrier as well. Two other runners accomplished the feat in a matter of weeks.

JOHN GARDNER
Excellence, p. 151

* * *

IF YOU BELIEVE IN ME

William James said, "Just as our courage is often a reflex of someone else's courage, so our faith is often a faith in someone else's faith." If you believe in me, it's easier for me to believe in myself.

JOHN GARDNER
Excellence, p. 151

* * *

FAITH IN HUMAN POSSIBILITIES

In leading, in teaching, in dealing with young people, in all relationships of influencing, directing, guiding, helping, nurturing, the whole tone of the relationship will be conditioned by our faith in human possibilities. That is the generative element, the source of the current that runs beneath the surface of such relationships.

JOHN GARDNER
Excellence, p. 151

COPING

THE BEST KEPT SECRET

I believe that most Americans would welcome a new burst of commitment. I do not believe the self-centeredness and disengagement of which they are accused is their natural state. *The best kept secret in America today is that people would rather work hard for something they believe in than live a life of aimless diversion.*

JOHN GARDNER
Excellence, p. 155

❋ ❋ ❋

THE PURSUIT OF EXCELLENCE

When we raise our sights, strive for excellence, dedicate ourselves to the highest goals of our society, we are enrolling in an ancient and meaningful cause — the age-long struggle of humans to realize the best that is in them. Humans reaching toward the most exalted goals they can conceive, striving impatiently and restlessly for excellence, have achieved religious insights, created works of art, penetrated secrets of the universe and set standards of conduct that heighten our sense of pride — and dignity as human beings.

JOHN GARDNER
Excellence, p. 160

EXCELLENCE

ON KEEPING A FREE SOCIETY FREE

Keeping a free society free—and vital and strong—is no job for
the half-educated and the slovenly. Men and women doing
capably whatever job is theirs to do tone up the whole society.
And those who do a slovenly job, whether they are janitors or
judges, surgeons or technicians, lower the tone of the society. So
do the chiselers of high and low degree, the sleight-of-hand artists
who always know how to gain an advantage without honest work.
They are burdens on a free society.

JOHN GARDNER
Excellence, p. 161

✳ ✳ ✳

STRIVING FOR THE
HIGHEST STANDARDS

But excellence implies more than competence.
It implies a striving for the highest standards
in every phase of life. We need individual excellence in all its forms—in every kind of creative
endeavor, in politics, in education, in industry,
in our spiritual life—in short, universally.

JOHN GARDNER
Excellence, p. 161

COPING

INSISTING ON THE
HIGHEST STANDARDS OF PERFORMANCE

Those who are most deeply devoted to a democratic society must be precisely the ones who insist upon excellence, who insist that free men and women are capable of the highest standards of performance, who insist that a free society can be a great society in the richest sense of that phrase. The idea for which this nation stands will not survive if the highest goal free citizens can set themselves is an amiable mediocrity.

JOHN GARDNER
Excellence, pp. 161–62

* * *

NOURISHING THE MONUMENTS OF THE SPIRIT

Unlike the great pyramids, the monuments of the spirit will not stand untended. They must be nourished in each generation by the allegiance of believing men and women. Free men and women, in their work, their family life, and in their public behavior should see themselves as builders and maintainers of the values of their society. Individual Americans—bus drivers and editors, grocers and senators, beauty parlor operators and ballplayers—can contribute to the greatness and strength of a free society—or they can help it die.

JOHN GARDNER
Excellence, p. 162

CRISIS OF CONSCIENCE

Modern-day managers are often faced with situations where they are required to commit themselves, either openly or tacitly, to an action they may not agree with. They may be participating, willingly or unwillingly, in activities that are morally and ethically cloudy; questionable from a business point of view; and, perhaps, of doubtful legality.

JOHN FENDROCK
"Crisis of Conscience at Quasar"

* * *

ETHICAL QUESTIONS

As corporate America struggles in a business environment that grows increasingly complex, managers are confronted with a rapidly expanding list of ethical questions that defy easy solutions. Should a company "absorb" new technology presented by a potential supplier who ultimately loses a bid to do business? What ethical responsibilities must a multinational corporation assume in a host country? Should the managers of a foreign subsidiary compromise their code of ethics to adapt to a new business environment? How does a manager balance the needs of his company with those of a loyal employee who suddenly develops a case of chronic absenteeism?

ROBERT GILBREATH
"The Hollow Executive"

COPING

CONFLICT IN VALUES

The manager has to live with a life in which he never really gets the luxury of choosing between right and wrong. He has to decide usually between two wrongs. In any decision he makes, he hurts somebody. And that's his career. If he's too uncomfortable with that, he ought to be in some other business. Obviously he ought to be uncomfortable with it. If he isn't uncomfortable, he's not very human.

J. IRWIN MILLER
(in Freudberg, p. 202)

* * *

THE NATURE OF DILEMMAS

The rule that it is best to tell the truth often runs up against the rule that we should not hurt people's feelings unncessarily. There is no simple, universal formula for solving ethical problems. We have to choose from our own codes of conduct whichever rules are appropriate to the case in hand; the outcome of those choices makes us who we are.

SIR ADRIAN CADBURY
"Ethical Managers Make Their Own Rules"

INTEGRITY

THE MORAL CLIMATE

In any community, some people are more or less irretrievably bad and others more or less consistently good. But the behavior of most people is profoundly influenced by the moral climate of the moment. One of the leader's tasks is to help ensure the soundness of that moral climate.

JOHN GARDNER
On Leadership, p. 192

* * *

LEADERS AND ETHICS

The leader is responsible for the set of ethics or norms that govern the behavior of people in the organization. Leaders can establish a set of ethics in several ways. One is to demonstrate by their own behavior their commitment to the set of ethics that they are trying to institutionalize. . . . Leaders set the moral tone by choosing carefully the people with whom they surround themselves, by communicating a sense of purpose for the organization, by reinforcing appropriate behaviors, and by articulating these moral positions to external and internal constituencies.

WARREN BENNIS and BURT NANUS
Leaders, p. 186

COPING

THE IMPORTANCE OF MORAL LEADERSHIP

I'm a great believer that leadership, in a large part, is moral leadership. And people want to follow moral leadership. They respect it. And they expect it too.

THORNTON BRADSHAW
(in Freudberg, p. 227)

* * *

THE MANAGER'S STYLE

In management, as in music, there is a base clef as well as a treble. The treble generally carries the melody in music, and melody's equivalent in management is the manager's style. A manager's style — the way he focuses his attention and interacts with people — sets the "tune" for his subordinates and communicates at the *operational* level what his expectations are and how he wants business conducted.

RICHARD PASCALE and ANTHONY ATHOS
The Art of Japanese Management, p. 177

THE GOOD LIFE

It is not a trivial question, Socrates said: What we are talking about is how one should live. . . . Once constituted in that way, it very naturally moves from the question, asked by anybody, "how should I live?" to the question "how should anybody live?" That seems to ask for the reasons we all share for living one way rather than another. It seems to ask for the conditions of *the good life*—the right life, perhaps, for human beings as such.

BERNARD WILLIAMS
Ethics and the Limits of Philosophy, p. 20

✳ ✳ ✳

A MATTER OF PERSPECTIVE

Ethics is, first of all, the quest for, and the understanding of, the good life, living well, a life worth living. It is largely a matter of *perspective*: putting every activity and goal in its place, knowing what is worth doing and what is not worth doing, knowing what is worth wanting and having and knowing what is not worth wanting and having.

ROBERT SOLOMON and KRISTINE HANSON
Above the Bottom Line, p. 9

COPING

INTEGRITY

Integrity relates to a way of knowing and thinking. As a synthesizing form of thought, executive integrity acts to preserve the whole by accepting polarities, appreciating differences, and finding connections that transcend and encompass all points of view.

SURESH SRIVASTVA and DAVID COOPERRIDER
"The Urgency for Executive Integrity"
(in Srivastva and Associates, p. 27)

✳ ✳ ✳

PERSONAL INTEGRITY

Personal integrity implies a firm adherence to a system of ethics, a set of guiding beliefs that are gradually forged by each individual and repeatedly tested in the crucible of one's own life. The wholeness of integrity demands, moreover, an integrated consistency of values, not the use of one set in the workplace and another at home. This implies an inner moral compass, a constancy, a conscience. This inner alarm is critical to long-term success as an executive.

THOMAS HORTON
"What Works for Me," p. 398

THE MORAL DIMENSION

The moral dimension finds its expression in the day-to-day behavior of the executive and, as such, is best illustrated by such behaviors as:

1. Establishing organizational values and goals that are realistic and strike a proper balance between the needs of the individual and the organization, and between the organization and the larger society.

2. Saying what you mean and consistently doing as you say.

3. Exemplifying high standards of ethics and performance and holding others accountable for similar standards.

4. Placing the needs of the whole before one's own ends and expecting the same of subordinates.

EDWARD GIBLAN
"The Road to Managerial Wisdom"

* * *

RIGHT DECISIONS

My basic principle is that you don't make decisions because they are easy, you don't make them because they are cheap, you don't make them because they are popular; you make them because they are right. Not distinguishing between rightness and wrongness is where administrators get into trouble.

FATHER THEODORE HESBURGH
(in Horton, p. 172)

COPING

A CHOICE OF ETHICAL SYSTEMS

When a businessman, or any person living in this complex and highly developed stage of civilization, tries to be ethical, he has a much more difficult task than is usually assumed. He has to choose which set of ethics he is going to employ. He has to make decisions, not merely between the good and the bad in a popular sense, but between various kinds of goodness as well, to determine their appropriateness in the total situation of which he is a part.

SAMUEL MILLER
"The Tangle of Ethics"

* * *

THE REQUIREMENT FOR ACTION

Excellent companies do more than talk ethics. They take positive steps to address ethical issues and apply the practical tools of ethics in their management practice. The application of ethics does not require that managers abdicate their responsibilities or turn the company into a debating society. Instead, integrating ethics helps managers to work more effectively and improve overall performance in their organizations.

MARK PASTIN
"Ethics and Excellence"

A STRATEGY FOR ETHICAL DECISION MAKING

Most successful corporations have discovered that decision making is most effective when supported by a strategy. Each choice is tested by asking: Does it contribute to the overriding strategy? . . . An ethical framework is no more than a personal strategy in this regard. Countless questions about a decision's immediate and ultimate consequences can be avoided by testing each alternative this way: Does it fit my ethical framework?

ROBERT GILBREATH
"The Hollow Executive"

* * *

THE NEED FOR STEADINESS

One of the most important prerequisites for trust in a leader is steadiness. The need for reliability is not only ethically desirable, it is generally a practical necessity. A leader who is unpredictable poses a nerve-wracking problem for followers. They cannot rally around a leader if they do not know where he or she stands. A businessman friend of mine, commenting on his congressman, said, "It isn't that he's crooked, it's just that I can't keep track of him. He's too swift for me—I wish he'd stay in one place."

JOHN GARDNER
On Leadership, p. 33

COPING

THE NEED FOR FAIRNESS

For leaders seeking to win trust, another requirement is fairness—fairness when the issues are being openly adjudicated, and, equally important, fairness in the backroom. Contending elements seek private access to the leader, and if it is widely believed that such offstage maneuvering works, the system is in a constant turmoil of suspicion. Nothing is more surely stabilizing than confidence that the leader is unshakably fair in private as well as in public.

JOHN GARDNER
On Leadership, p. 33

✳ ✳ ✳

BEYOND STANDARD MANAGEMENT TOOLS

The box of standard management tools does not include the powerful tools of ethics. By adding ethics to the box of management tools, managers can view these problems in a new light and use ethics to gain competitive edges over ethics-blind competitors.

MARK PASTIN
The Hard Problems of Management, p. 2

THINKING "OUTSIDE THE BOX"

To think in ethical terms is to think "outside the box." The box in question is the box of standard tools of management thinking. The very factors that give prominence to ethics in business also make standard business tools irrelevant to the nonstandard problems that managers regularly confront. These factors mark a fundamental change in the business environment.

MARK PASTIN
The Hard Problems of Management, p. 5

✻ ✻ ✻

THE NATURE OF TRUST

Trust is the ultimate intangible. It has no shape or substance, yet it empowers our actions. And its presence or absence can govern our behavior as if it were a tangible force. . . . Trust is the "miracle ingredient" in organizational life—a lubricant that reduces friction, a bonding agent that glues together disparate parts, a catalyst that facilitates action. No substitute—neither threat nor promise—will do the job as well.

GORDON SHEA
Building Trust in the Workplace, p. 13, p. 21

COPING

THE REWARDS OF POSITIVE REPUTATION

The rewards of positive reputation are realized in a variety of ways. Having our opinion sought communicates respect; being invited to participate in a significant meeting, being trusted with confidential information, being thanked for the role played behind the scenes are ways which people use to tell us we have built a reputation.

RICHARD PASCALE and ANTHONY ATHOS
The Art of Japanese Management, p. 143

* * *

THE NEED FOR RIGHT-GOOD DECISIONS

The notion that nice guys finish last is not only poisonous but wrong. In fact, the contrary is true. Unethical conduct is always self-destructive and generates more unethical conduct until you hit the pits. The challenge is not always being ethical or paying a big price. The challenge is to be ethical and get what you want. I think you can do it almost every time.

MICHAEL JOSEPHSON
Time, May 25, 1987

IV

Knowing

We live in an age of affluence in many respects.
The mass media bombard us with stimuli and
we have to protect ourselves by filtering them,
as it were. We are offered a lot of possibilities
and have to make our choices among them.
In short, we have to make decisions as
to what is essential and what is not.

VIKTOR FRANKL
The Will to Meaning, p. 65

✳

Knowing Oneself

Knowing the Job

Knowing the Organization

Knowing the Business One Is In

Knowing the World

Knowing Oneself

THE SELF-RENEWING PERSON

For the self-renewing person the development of his or her own potentialities and the process of self-discovery never end. It is a sad but unarguable fact that most human beings go through their lives only partially aware of the full range of their abilities.

JOHN GARDNER
Self-Renewal, p. 10

* * *

ON KNOWING ONESELF

One must know oneself before knowing anything else. It is only after a man has thus understood himself inwardly and has thus seen his way, that life acquires peace and significance.

SÖREN KIERKEGAARD
The Journals (in Bretall, p. 6)

STRANGERS TO OURSELVES

We are unknown to ourselves, we men of knowledge — and with good reason. We have never sought ourselves — how could it happen that we should ever *find* ourselves? . . . So we are necessarily strangers to ourselves, we do not comprehend ourselves, we *have* to misunderstand ourselves, for us the law "Each is furthest from himself" applies to all eternity — we are not "men of knowledge" with respect to ourselves.

FRIEDRICH NIETZSCHE
On the Genealogy of Morals,
(in Kaufmann, p. 451)

✳ ✳ ✳

PROTECTION OF OUR SELF-ESTEEM

In general this fear of knowledge is defensive, in the sense that it is a protection of our self-esteem, of our love and respect for ourselves. We tend to be afraid of any knowledge that could cause us to despise ourselves or to make us feel inferior, weak, worthless, evil, shameful. We protect ourselves and our ideal image of ourselves by repression and similar defenses, which are essentially techniques by which we avoid becoming conscious of unpleasant or dangerous truths.

ABRAHAM MASLOW
Toward a Psychology of Being, p. 5

TWO ASPECTS OF RESISTANCE

When the mature person changes, he does so against a natural resistance; but whether this resistance is a deeply stabilizing influence that helps him to retain his basic direction and character, or whether it is a cocoon that makes him unreachable, is a moot question. Resistance, though built in, may thus be either a roadblock or a gyroscope.

PAUL BROUWER
"The Power to See Ourselves"

* * *

THE SELF-CONCEPT AS FILTER

Photographers often slip a reddish filter over the lens when snapping pictures of clouds on black and white film. The filter prevents some of the light rays from reaching the film, so that the final picture shows much darker skies and more sharply whitened clouds. The self-concept is like a filter that screens out what we do not want to hear and see, passes through what we do want to see and hear.

PAUL BROUWER
"The Power to See Ourselves"

FEAR OF KNOWLEDGE

From our point of view, Freud's greatest discovery is that the great cause of much psychological illness is the fear of knowledge of oneself—of one's emotions, impulses, memories, capacities, potentialities, of one's destiny. We have discovered that fear of knowledge of oneself is very often isomorphic with, and parallel with, fear of the outside world. That is, inner problems and outer problems tend to be deeply similar and to be related to each other. Therefore we speak simply of fear of knowledge in general, without discriminating too sharply fear-of-the-inner from fear-of-the-outer.

ABRAHAM MASLOW
Toward a Psychology of Being, p. 5

✳ ✳ ✳

KNOWING AND DOING

This close relation between knowing and doing can help us to interpret one cause of the fear of knowing as deeply a fear of doing, a fear of the consequences that flow from knowing, a fear of its dangerous responsibilities. Often it is better not to know, because if you *did* know, then you would *have* to act and stick your neck out. This is a little involved, a little like the man who said, "I'm so glad I don't like oysters. Because if I liked oysters, I'd eat them, and I *hate* the darned things."

ABRAHAM MASLOW
Toward a Psychology of Being, p. 66

DENYING OUR TALENTS

But there is another kind of truth we tend to evade. Not only do we hang on to our psychopathology, but also we tend to evade personal growth because this, too, can bring another kind of fear, of awe, of feelings of weakness and inadequacy. And so we find another kind of resistance, a denying of our best side, of our talents, of our finest impulses, of our highest potentialities, of our creativeness. In brief this is the struggle against our own greatness, the fear of *hubris* (i.e., arrogance).

ABRAHAM MASLOW
Toward a Psychology of Being, p. 61

* * *

HOW TO VIEW YOURSELF

If a person believes himself to be weak, helpless, or doomed to some fate or other, he will tend to behave or suffer in the way expected. If, on the other hand, he has a concept of himself as a being with much untapped potential to cope with problems and contradictions in his life, then when they arise, he will persist in efforts to cope with them long after someone who sees himself as ineffective and impotent has given up.

SIDNEY JOURARD
Disclosing Man to Himself, p. 217

CHANGE IN SELF-CONCEPT

A psychological fact is that manager development means change in the manager's self-concept. Each of us, whether we realize it or not, has a self-image. We see ourselves in some way—smart, slow, kindly, well-intentioned, lazy, misunderstood, meticulous, or shrewd; we all can pick adjectives that describe ourselves. This is the "I" behind the face in the mirror, the "I" that thinks, dreams, talks, and believes, the "I" that no one knows fully.

PAUL BROUWER
"The Power to See Ourselves"

✳ ✳ ✳

KNOW THYSELF

"Know thyself" was the inscription over the Oracle at Delphi. And it is still the most difficult task any of us faces. But until you truly know yourself, strengths and weaknesses, know what you want to do and why you want to do it, you cannot succeed in any but the most superficial sense of the word. The leader never lies to himself, especially about himself, knows his flaws as well as his assets, and deals with them directly. You are your own raw material. When you know what you consist of and what you want to make of it, then you can invent yourself.

WARREN BENNIS
On Becoming a Leader, p. 40

KNOWING ONESELF

ON SELF-KNOWLEDGE

After you get over the pain, eventually self-knowledge is a very nice thing. It feels good to know about something rather than to wonder about it, to speculate about it.

ABRAHAM MASLOW
"Synanon and Eupsychia"

* * *

THE VALUE OF CRITICISM

The person who is criticized honestly may be hurt for the moment, but ultimately he is helped and cannot help but become grateful. Anyway, it's a great sign of respect to me, for instance, if someone feels I'm strong enough, capable enough, and objective enough so that he or she can tell me when I've pulled a boner.

ABRAHAM MASLOW
Eupsychian Management, p. 163

ON OBTAINING FEEDBACK

I have asked hundreds of managers this question: If you engage in behaviors that create problems for the people who work with you and for you, would you like to know what these behaviors are? As you might guess, more than 90 percent respond that they would indeed like to have such information. Then I ask a second question: How many of you have a method you feel good about for obtaining such data? Less than 25 percent indicate that they have any process for getting such feedback. Why this great disparity between the desire for feedback and the inability or unwillingness to gather it?

WILLIAM DYER
*Contemporary Issues in Management
and Organization Development*, p. 147

* * *

ON SELF-EXAMINATION

The function of self-examination is to lay the groundwork for insight, without which no growth can occur. Insight is the "Oh, I see now" feeling which must, consciously or unconsciously, precede change in behavior. Insights — real, genuine glimpses of ourselves as we really are — are reached only with difficulty and sometimes with real psychic pain. But they are the building blocks of growth. Thus self-examination is a preparation for insight, a groundbreaking for the seeds of self-understanding which gradually bloom into changed behavior.

PAUL BROUWER
"The Power to See Ourselves"

REALISM AND EFFECTIVENESS

Unfortunately, not only outright failure may come from disparities in self-concept; more insidious is the effect of partial or fuzzy self-appraisal. In fact, if the proposition is right that realism in the individual's view of himself has a one-to-one relationship with effectiveness on the job, then it surely follows that all of us can improve our effectiveness by the simple expedient of developing a more realistic, more accurate self-concept!

PAUL BROUWER
"The Power to See Ourselves"

* * *

KNOWING WHAT
YOU DO NOT KNOW

Well, I am certainly wiser than this man. It is only too likely that neither of us has any knowledge to boast of, but he thinks that he knows something which he does not know, whereas I am quite conscious of my ignorance. At any rate it seems that I am wiser than he is to this small extent, that I do not think that I know what I do not know.

SOCRATES
"Apology"
(in Hamilton and Cairns, pp. 7–8)

SEEING OUR POTENTIAL

It is not enough, however, just to see ourselves as we are now. Such understanding is a necessary starting point, or basis on which to build. But we must also see what our real selves could be, and grow into that.

PAUL BROUWER
"The Power to See Ourselves"

Knowing the Job

DEFINING THE JOB

Logically it is inconceivable that any individual should be appointed to a position carrying a large salary, without a clear idea of the part which that position is meant to play in the general social pattern of which it is a component, the responsibilities and relationships attached to it, and the standard of performance which is expected in return for the expenditure. It is as illogical as to attempt to order an expensive piece of machinery without a specification.

LYNDALL URWICK
"Scientific Principles and Organization"

* * *

POSITION DESCRIPTIONS

Every managerial position should be defined. A good position description informs the incumbent and others what he or she is supposed to do. A modern position description is not a detailed list of all the activities a manager is expected to undertake and it certainly does not specify *how* to undertake them. Rather, it states the basic function of the position, the major end-result areas for which the manager is responsible, the reporting relationships involved, and makes reference to the current chart of approval authorizations for clarifying the position's authority and the current set of verifiable objectives in effect.

KOONTZ, O'DONNELL, and WEIHRICH
Management, p. 490

THE OBJECTIVE OF EACH POSITION

There are many position descriptions in rather common use which do not contain an overall statement of objective. The objective of a position should be a brief statement of conditions that will exist or the results that will be attained if the job is done satisfactorily. They are conditions and results which would not be brought about if the position did not exist or the functions of the position were not performed. The absence of careful thought in the preparation of position objectives leads to overemphasis of procedures without proper attention to their contribution to the end desired.

LAWRENCE APPLEY
Management in Action, p. 186

* * *

REQUIREMENT FOR AN ORGANIZATIONAL ROLE

For an organizational role to exist and to be meaningful to people, it must incorporate (1) verifiable objectives; (2) a clear concept of the major duties or activities involved; and (3) an understood area of discretion, or authority, so that the person filling it knows what he or she can do to accomplish results. In addition, to make a role operational, provision should be made for needed information and other tools and resources necessary for performance in a role.

KOONTZ, O'DONNELL, and WEIHRICH
Management, p. 330

KNOWING THE JOB

AN OPEN-ENDED JOB

Why do managers adopt this (unrelenting) pace and workload? One major reason is the inherently open-ended nature of their job. Managers are responsible for the success of their organization, and there are really no tangible mileposts where they can stop and say, "Now my job is finished." The engineer finishes the design on a casting on a certain day, the lawyer wins or loses the case at some moment in time. Managers must always keep going, never sure when they have succeeded, never sure when their whole organization may come down around them because of some miscalculation. As a result, managers are persons with a perpetual preoccupation.

HENRY MINTZBERG
The Nature of Managerial Work, p. 30

✳ ✳ ✳

THE BASIC JOB OF MANAGEMENT

The overall profit made by a company is merely the sum total of the individual efforts of its many employees. The more individuals in the organization who are producing more than they consume, the greater the profit of the organization and of the individuals in it. The basic job of management, therefore, is to increase the value of the contribution of all members of the organization or, in other words, to increase their productivity.

LAWRENCE APPLEY
Management in Action, p. 218

THE WORK OF THE MANAGER

There are five basic operations in the work of managers. Together they result in the integration of resources into a viable growing organism.

1. Managers, in the first place, set objectives. They determine what the objectives should be. They decide what has to be done to reach these objectives.

2. Second, managers organize. They analyze the activities, decisions, and relations needed. They classify the work.

3. Next, managers motivate and communicate. They make a team out of the people who are responsible for various jobs.

4. The fourth basic element in the work of managers is measurement. Managers establish yardsticks. They analyze, appraise, and interpret performance.

5. Finally, managers develop people, including themselves.

PETER DRUCKER
Management, p. 400

THE ESSENTIALS OF EFFECTIVENESS

1. Effective executives work systematically at managing their time.

2. Effective executives focus on outward contribution.

3. Effective executives build on strengths.

4. Effective executives concentrate on the few major areas where superior performance will produce outstanding results.

5. Effective executives, finally, make effective decisions.

PETER DRUCKER
The Effective Executive, pp. 23–24

✳ ✳ ✳

WHAT CAN I CONTRIBUTE?

The effective executive focuses on contribution. He looks up from his work and outward toward goals. He asks: "What can I contribute that will significantly affect the performance and the results of the institution I serve?" His stress is on responsibility. . . . He holds himself accountable for the performance of the whole.

PETER DRUCKER
The Effective Executive, pp. 52–53

ON MAKING BEAUTIFUL MUSIC

For corporate players to make beautiful music together they must achieve a balance between concentrating on their own areas of skill and responsibility and working together with others. They need to do their own jobs well while keeping one eye on what might be useful for someone else. They need to understand enough about the company's other areas to identify possibilities for joint action and mutual enhancement. They need to simultaneously focus and collaborate. They must function in many roles: as soloist, ensemble players, and members of the orchestra.

ROSABETH MOSS KANTER
When Giants Learn to Dance, p. 116

* * *

AN INCREASE IN COMPLEXITY

Post-entrepreneurial organizations vastly increase the complexities that managers and professionals deal with and multiply the responsibilities that they bear. After all, they are no longer simply following established procedures or working solely within their own circumscribed area; they are also developing joint projects with other units in pursuit of synergies, and they are coordinating closely with customers, suppliers, and other external partners. The more integrated and synergistic the organization, the more time is spent in communication.

ROSABETH MOSS KANTER
When Giants Learn to Dance, p. 276

OPPORTUNITIES FOR CREATING THE JOB

While traditional, perhaps more bureaucratic, managerial jobs are being eliminated at a record rate, and managers face growing career uncertainty, changes in the content of jobs provide new kinds of opportunities. . . . In the workplace that is emerging as companies gear up for the global corporate Olympics, opportunity goes to those who can *create* the job, not those who inherit a predetermined set of tasks defining a hierarchical position.

ROSABETH MOSS KANTER
When Giants Learn to Dance, p. 304

❋ ❋ ❋

UNCERTAINTY ABOUT CAREER PATHS

While full of opportunity, this new workplace style is also full of uncertainty. The very chance to invent, shape, or grow a job puts career responsibility squarely in the hands of the individual. If jobs are fluid and created by their incumbents, how can organizations define orderly career paths?

ROSABETH MOSS KANTER
When Giants Learn to Dance, p. 305

❋ ❋ ❋

UPWARD MOBILITY BASED UPON SKILL

Opportunity in the professional form involves the chance to take on ever-more-demanding or challenging or important or rewarding assignments that require greater exercise of the skills that are the professional's stock in trade. "Upward mobility" in the professional career rests on the reputation for greater skill.

ROSABETH MOSS KANTER
When Giants Learn to Dance, p. 310

POWER OF THE PERSON

Overall, the power of the position is giving way to the power of the person. A formal title and its placement on an organization chart have less to do with career prospects and career success in a post-entrepreneurial world than the skills and ideas a person brings to that work. The model can produce world-class athletes in Olympic contests for corporations that know how to develop and tap skills, wherever they are found. This model can open vast opportunities for people as well, if the training, coaching, and financial backing are available to help them move with their skills and their ideas.

ROSABETH MOSS KANTER
When Giants Learn to Dance, pp. 318–19

✳ ✳ ✳

ON FACING REALITY

The point is, what determines your destiny is not the hand you're dealt; it's how you play the hand. And the best way to play your hand is to face reality—see the world the way it is— and act accordingly.

JACK WELCH
"Speed, Simplicity, Self-Confidence"
(by Noel Tichy and Ram Charan)

Knowing the Organization

THE BUSINESS ORGANIZATION
AS A SOCIAL SYSTEM

The firm is a society, and the individual lives in it. When the firm is viewed as a social system, it is recognized that the value dimension of business is involved in every act of the individuals who make up that society. Certainly, it is the individuals within the social system of the firm who are most affected by the values of the firm and do most to create the firm's values. Thus, we cannot ignore the fact that business itself is a value-forging social system for its members.

ALVAR ELBING and CAROL ELBING
The Value Issue of Business, p. 94

* * *

UNDERSTANDING THE CULTURE

It is important for all managers—or employees for that matter—to have a good and precise sense of the culture of their companies. Once you know more exactly the type of culture that you're dealing with, you will have a better idea of how to get things done in an effective way.

TERRENCE DEAL and ALLAN KENNEDY
Corporate Cultures, p. 127

THE MEANING OF CORPORATE CULTURE

Corporate culture is the pattern of shared beliefs and values that give the members of an institution meaning, and provide them with the rules for behavior in their organization. Every organization will have its own word or phrase to describe what it means by culture; some of these are: being, core, culture, ethos, identity, ideology, manner, patterns, philosophy, purpose, roots, spirit, style, vision, and way. To most managers, these mean pretty much the same thing.

STANLEY DAVIS
Managing Corporate Culture, p. 1

* * *

THE NATURE OF VALUES

Values are the basic concepts and beliefs of an organization; as such they form the heart of the corporate culture. Values define "success" in concrete terms for employees—"if you do this, you too will be a success"—and establish standards of achievement within the organization. The strong culture companies that we investigated all had a rich and complex system of values that were shared by the employees. Managers in these companies talked about these beliefs openly and without embarrassment, and they didn't tolerate deviance from the company standards.

TERRENCE DEAL and ALLAN KENNEDY
Corporate Cultures, p. 14

KNOWING THE ORGANIZATION

PROVIDING A COMMON DIRECTION

Values are the bedrock of any corporate culture. As the essence of a company's philosophy for achieving success, values provide a sense of common direction for all employees and guidelines for their day-to-day behavior. These formulas for success determine the types of corporate heroes, and the myths, rituals, and ceremonies of the culture. In fact, we think that often companies succeed because their employees can identify, embrace, and act on the values of the organization.

TERRENCE DEAL and ALLAN KENNEDY
Corporate Cultures, p. 21

* * *

A SENSE OF IDENTITY

For those who hold them, shared values define the fundamental character of their organization, the attitude that distinguishes it from all others. In this way, they create a sense of identity for those in the organization, making employees feel special. Moreover, values are a reality in the minds of most people throughout the company, not just the senior executives. It is this sense of pulling together that makes shared values so effective.

TERRENCE DEAL and ALLAN KENNEDY
Corporate Cultures, p. 23

THE DIFFICULTY OF DEALING WITH VALUES

"Rational" managers rarely pay much attention to the value system of an organization. Values are not "hard," like organizational structures, policies and procedures, strategies, or budgets. Often they are not even written down. And when someone does try to set them down in a formal statement of corporate philosophy, the product often bears an uncomfortable resemblance to the Biblical beatitudes—good and true and broadly constructive, but not all that relevant on Monday morning.

TERRENCE DEAL and ALLAN KENNEDY
Corporate Cultures, p. 21

* * *

GUIDING BELIEFS AND DAILY BELIEFS

Guiding beliefs are the roots and principles upon which the company is built, the philosophical foundation of the corporation. As fundamental precepts, guiding beliefs rarely change. They are held in the realm of universal truths, and are broad enough to accommodate any variety of circumstances.

Daily beliefs, on the other hand, are a different species. While they are equally part of a corporation's culture, they should not be confused with guiding beliefs. Daily beliefs are rules and feelings about everyday behavior. They are situational and change to meet circumstances. They tell people the ropes to skip and the ropes to know. They are the survival kit for the individual.

STANLEY DAVIS
Managing Corporate Culture, p. 4

BELIEVING IN SOMETHING

We were talking about the problems of organizations, and someone asked, "What makes for consistently outstanding company performance?" Another person offered the hypothesis that the companies that did best over the long haul were those that believed in something. The example was, "IBM means service."

TERRENCE DEAL and ALLAN KENNEDY
Corporate Cultures, p. 6

✳ ✳ ✳

HEALTHY COMPANIES
AND GUIDING BELIEFS

With truly healthy companies, everyone—employees, customers, shareholders, competitors, government, and the public at large—knows what the company stands for. Employees, especially, have the guiding beliefs in the forefront of their minds, and are able to apply them easily to their daily behavior.

STANLEY DAVIS
Managing Corporate Culture, p. 4

KNOWING

CHARACTERISTICS OF SUCCESSFUL COMPANIES

- They stand for something—that is, they have a clear and explicit philosophy about how they aim to conduct their business.
- Management pays a great deal of attention to shaping and fine-tuning these values to conform to the economic and business environment of the company and to communicating them to the organization.
- These values are known and shared by all the people who work for the company—from the lowliest production worker right through the ranks of senior management.

TERRENCE DEAL and ALLAN KENNEDY
Corporate Cultures, p. 22

* * *

SIGNS OF A CULTURE IN TROUBLE

- Weak cultures have no clear values or beliefs about how to succeed in their business; or
- They have many such beliefs but cannot agree among themselves on which are most important; or
- Different parts of the company have fundamentally different beliefs.
- The heroes of the culture are destructive or disruptive and don't build upon any common understanding about what is important.
- The rituals of day-to-day life are either disorganized—with everybody doing their own thing—or downright contradictory—with the left hand and the right hand working at cross purposes.

TERRENCE DEAL and ALLAN KENNEDY
Corporate Cultures, pp. 135–36

THE STRONG CULTURE

A strong culture is a system of informal rules that spells out how people are to behave most of the time. By knowing what exactly is expected of them, employees will waste little time in deciding how to act in a given situation. . . . The impact of a strong culture on productivity is amazing. In the extreme, we estimate that a company can gain as much as one or two hours of productive work per employee per day.

TERRENCE DEAL and ALLAN KENNEDY
Corporate Cultures, p. 15

✳ ✳ ✳

HOW SHARED VALUES AFFECT PERFORMANCE

- Managers and others throughout the organization give extraordinary attention to whatever matters are stressed in the corporate value system.

- Down-the-line managers make marginally better decisions, on average, because they are guided by their perception of the shared values.

- People simply work a little harder because they are dedicated to the cause.

TERRENCE DEAL and ALLAN KENNEDY
Corporate Cultures, p. 33

PEOPLE MAKE BUSINESSES WORK

American business needs to return to the original concepts and ideas that made institutions like NCR, General Electric, IBM, Procter & Gamble, 3M, and others great. We need to remember that people make businesses work. And we need to relearn old lessons about how culture ties people together and gives meaning and purpose to their day-to-day lives.

TERRENCE DEAL and ALLAN KENNEDY
Corporate Cultures, p. 5

* * *

STRONG CULTURE COMPANIES

The future holds promise for strong culture companies. Strong cultures are not only able to respond to an environment, but they also adapt to diverse and changing circumstances. When times are tough, these companies can reach deeply into their shared values and beliefs for the truth and courage to see them through. When new challenges arise, they can adjust. This is exactly what companies are going to have to do as we begin to experience a revolution in the structure of modern organizations.

TERRENCE DEAL and ALLAN KENNEDY
Corporate Cultures, pp. 195–96

Knowing the Business One Is In

AN ORGAN OF SOCIETY

An organization is not, like an animal, an end in itself, and successful by the mere act of perpetuating the species. An organization is an organ of society and fulfills itself by the contribution it makes to the outside environment. And yet the bigger and apparently more successful an organization gets to be, the more will inside events tend to engage the interests, the energies, and the abilities of the executive to the exclusion of his real tasks and his real effectiveness in the outside.

PETER DRUCKER
The Effective Executive, pp. 15–16

❋ ❋ ❋

THE BUSINESS ENVIRONMENT

Each company faces a different reality in the marketplace depending on its products, competitors, customers, technologies, government influences, and so on. To succeed in its marketplace, each company must carry out certain kinds of activities very well. In some markets that means selling; in others, invention; in still others, management of costs. In short, the environment in which a company operates determines what it must do to be a success. This business environment is the single greatest influence in shaping a corporate culture.

TERRENCE DEAL and ALLAN KENNEDY
Corporate Cultures, p. 13

KNOWING

WHAT IS OUR BUSINESS?

That business purpose and business mission are so rarely given adequate thought is perhaps the most important single cause of business frustration and business failure. Conversely, in outstanding businesses . . . success always rests to a large extent on raising the question "What is our business?" clearly and deliberatively, and on answering it thoughtfully and thoroughly.

PETER DRUCKER
Management, p. 78

* * *

A CHALLENGING QUESTION

Nothing may seem simpler or more obvious than to answer what a company's business is. A steel mill makes steel, a railroad runs trains to carry freight and passengers, an insurance company underwrites fire risks. Indeed, the question looks so simple that it is seldom raised, the answer seems so obvious that it is seldom given. . . . Actually "what is our business" is almost always a difficult question which can be answered only after hard thinking and studying. And the right answer is usually anything but obvious.

PETER DRUCKER
The Practice of Management, p. 49

KNOWING THE BUSINESS ONE IS IN

"WHAT SHOULD OUR BUSINESS BE?"

But there is need also to ask "What *should* our business be?" What opportunities are opening up or can be created to fulfill the purpose and mission of the business by making it into a *different* business?

PETER DRUCKER
Management, p. 92

❋ ❋ ❋

IMPORTANCE OF THE CUSTOMER

It is the customer who determines what a business is. For it is the customer, and he alone, who through being willing to pay for a good or for a service, converts economic resources into wealth, things into goods. What the business thinks it produces is not of first importance—especially not to the future of the business and to its success. What the customer thinks he is buying, what he considers "value," is decisive—it determines what a business is, what it produces and whether it will prosper. . . . The customer is the foundation of a business and keeps it in existence.

PETER DRUCKER
The Practice of Management, p. 37

WHAT IS VALUE TO THE CUSTOMER

With respect to the definition of business purpose and business mission, there is only one
such focus, one starting point. It is the customer. The customer defines the business. . . .
The final question needed to come to grips
with business purpose and business mission is:
"What is value to the customer?" It may be the
most important question. Yet it is the one least
often asked.

PETER DRUCKER
Management, p. 79, p. 83

✳ ✳ ✳

BUSINESS STRATEGIES FOR TOMORROW

Any institution needs to think strategically what its business is
doing and what it should be doing. It needs to think through what
its customers pay it for. What is "value" for *our* customers? . . .
Every institution needs to think through what its strengths are.
Are they the right strengths for its specific business? Are they
adequate? Are they deployed where they will produce results?
And what specifically is the "market" for this particular business,
both at the present time and in the years immediately ahead?

PETER DRUCKER
Managing in Turbulent Times, p. 61

IDENTIFYING THE VALUES

The question should be asked "What are the *values* that are truly important to us in the company?" It might be product or process safety. It might be product quality. It might be the ability of the company dealers to give proper service to the customer and so on. Whatever the values are, they have to be organizationally anchored. There has to be an organizational component responsible for them—and it has to be a key component.

PETER DRUCKER
Management, p. 531

* * *

FOCUSING ON STRENGTHS

Any business needs to know its strengths and to base its strategy on them. What do *we* do well? What are the areas in which *we* perform? Most businesses and public service institutions alike believe it possible to be a "leader" in every area. But strengths are always specific, always unique. One gets paid only for strengths; one does not get paid for weaknesses. The question, therefore, is first: 'What are our specific strengths?" And then: "Are they the right strengths?"

PETER DRUCKER
Managing in Turbulent Times, p. 65

THE IMPORTANCE OF CONCENTRATION

If there is any one "secret" of effectiveness, it is concentration. Effective executives do first things first and they do one thing at a time. . . . Concentration — that is, the courage to impose on time and events one's own decision as to what really matters and comes first — is the executive's only hope of becoming the master of time and events instead of their whipping boy.

PETER DRUCKER
The Effective Executive, p. 100, p. 112

* * *

SETTING PRIORITIES

No business can do everything. Even if it has the money, it will never have enough good people. It has to set priorities. The worst thing is to try to do a little bit of everything. This makes sure that nothing is being accomplished. It is better to pick the wrong priority than none at all.

PETER DRUCKER
Management, p. 119

KNOWING THE BUSINESS ONE IS IN

GUIDELINES FOR IDENTIFYING PRIORITIES

Courage rather than analysis dictates the truly important role for identifying priorities:

- Pick the future as against the past;

- Focus on opportunity rather than on problems;

- Choose your own direction—rather than climb on the bandwagon; and

- Aim high, aim for something that will make a difference, rather than for something that is "safe" and easy to do.

PETER DRUCKER
The Effective Executive, p. 111

✳ ✳ ✳

ON PROFITS

But what about a profit objective? The answer is that there has never been one (at Marks & Spencer). Obviously the company is highly profitable and highly profit conscious. But it sees profit not as an objective but as a requirement of the business, that is, not as a goal but as a need. Profit, in the Marks & Spencer view, is the result of doing things rather than the purpose of business activity. ... Profitability is a measurement of how well the business discharges its functions in serving market and customer.

PETER DRUCKER
Management, p. 98

NO APOLOGY NEEDED

No apology is needed for profit as a necessity of economy and society. On the contrary, what a businessman should feel guilty about, what he should feel the need to apologize for, is failure to produce a profit appropriate to the economic and social functions which profit, and only profit, can develop.

PETER DRUCKER
Management, p. 73

* * *

NEED FOR A SYSTEMS VIEW

A piecemeal approach will not suffice. To have a real understanding of the business of the business, the executive must be able to see it in its entirety. He must be able to see its resources and efforts as a whole and to see their allocation to products and services, to markets, customers, end-uses, to distributive channels. He must be able to see which efforts go onto problems and which onto opportunities. He must be able to weigh alternatives of direction and allocation. Partial analysis is likely to misinform and misdirect. Only the overall view of the entire business as an economic system can give real knowledge.

PETER DRUCKER
Managing for Results, p. 11

Knowing the World

ONLY US

The world has shrunk, and there no longer is a category of Them. There is only Us — gropers for challenge, growth, fulfillment and meaning in our lives. Some older, some younger; some enlightened, others mystified and befuddled. Some rich, some poor. Some of us will have to help the rest of the world get as rich as us.

SIDNEY JOURARD
Disclosing Man to Himself, p. 198

* * *

A SINGLE BODY

The world of humanity is meant to become a single body; but it is as yet nothing more than a heap of limbs, each of which is of the opinion that it constitutes an entire body. Furthermore, the human world is meant to become a single body through the actions of men themselves.

MARTIN BUBER
On Judaism, p. 182

MORE LIKE CORAL

I think we have trained a whole generation of people to think in terms of an isolated "I." But anyone like myself, trained in biology, knows that the human being is not like an amoeba, it's not a thing. We're much more like coral, we're interconnected. We cannot survive without each other.

WILLARD GAYLIN
(in Moyers, p. 119)

* * *

THE NEED FOR A GLOBAL PERSPECTIVE

The crucial question here, as I see it, is simply: With what society, what social group, do you identify yourself? Is it going to be with all the people of the planet, or is it going to be with your own particular in-group? This is the question, essentially, that was in the minds of the founders of our nation when the people of the thirteen states began thinking of themselves as of one nation, yet without losing consideration for the special interests of each of the several states. Why can't something of that kind take place in the world right now?

JOSEPH CAMPBELL
The Power of Myth, p. 182

KNOWING THE WORLD

ALL LINKED IN HUMANITY

Our basic problem is moral: to survive and to live well, and to be a conscious member of the family of man, aware that we are all linked in humanity, and thus able to utilize the instruments of science, technology, and the arts of society for universally worthwhile purposes.

PAUL KURTZ
The Fullness of Life, pp. 214–15

* * *

HUMANKIND MUST CHANGE

Whoever goes on living as before has not grasped the menace. Mere intellectual speculation about it does not mean absorption into the reality of one's life — and the life of man is lost without a change. Man must change if he wants to go on living. If he thinks only of today, a day will come when the outbreak of nuclear war is apt to finish everything.

KARL JASPERS
The Future of Mankind, p. 24

THE UNITY OF HUMANITY

Thousands of years ago mankind developed monotheism—the belief in one God. Today another step is due. I would call it monanthropism—the awareness of one mankind, the awareness of the unity of humanity; a unity in whose light the different colors of our skin would fade away.

VIKTOR FRANKL
The Will to Meaning, p. 98

* * *

TO BE CITIZENS OF THE WORLD

We have learned that we cannot live alone, at peace; that our own well-being is dependent on the well-being of other nations far away. We have learned that we must live as human beings, and not as ostriches, nor as dogs in the manger. We have learned to be citizens of the world, members of the human community.

FRANKLIN DELANO ROOSEVELT
Quotations from our Presidents, p. 51

A TWOFOLD CITIZENSHIP

Everybody today, with part of his being, belongs to one country, with its specific traditions and problems, while with another part he has become a citizen of a world which no longer permits national isolation. Seen in this light there could not be any conflict between nationalism and internationalism, between the nation and the world.

DAG HAMMARSKJÖLD
(in Kelen, p. 10)

* * *

TOWARD CIVILIZED CONCOURSE

There are different systems in the world. There are different nationalities, different cultures, different personalities. . . . But as long as you can say, "I am what I am, but that doesn't mean I'm better than anybody else; it means I'm different, and the other one is different too, and we can understand each other, we can talk, we can communicate" — that is the basic attitude that makes life civilized and diplomacy possible. That is the expression of civilized concourse between nations.

CARLOS FUENTES
(in Moyers, p. 513)

TRANSCENDING NATIONALISM

In every field we must aim to transcend nationalism: and the first step towards this is to think globally—how could this or that task be achieved by international cooperation rather than by separate action?

JULIAN HUXLEY
"The Humanist Frame" (in Huxley, p. 23)

* * *

ECONOMIC COOPERATION

There is a general conclusion to be drawn from modern economic development, and that is that any nation which desires to prosper must seek rather cooperation than competition with other nations. The world is economically unified in a way in which it never was at any earlier period.

BERTRAND RUSSELL
New Hopes for a Changing World, p. 139

* * *

A PRICE TO BE PAID

There is a price to be paid for organized international cooperation. But it is a far lesser price than the one that would be exacted from any nation that attempted in this day and generation to "go it alone."

DAG HAMMARSKJÖLD
(in Kelen, p. 12)

WORLD PEACE THROUGH WORLD TRADE

Instead of resisting increased economic interdependence, we should be embracing it wholeheartedly. In my view, it is our great hope for peace. If we get sufficiently interlaced economically, we will most probably *not* bomb each other off the face of the planet.

JOHN NAISBITT
Megatrends, p. 77

* * *

A UNITARY WHOLE

Today education can no longer foster merely the individual's self-fulfillment and the welfare of his country. A new curriculum must be developed: a curriculum which will perceive all mankind as a unitary whole.

JOSHUA WEINSTEIN
Buber and Humanistic Education, p. 91

* * *

THE REALLY VITAL QUESTION

The really vital question for us all is, What is this world going to be? What is life eventually to make of itself?

WILLIAM JAMES
Pragmatism, p. 86

KNOWING

THE NEED FOR WISDOM

In our own day a combination of scientific genius and technical skill has produced the atomic bomb, but having produced it we are all terrified, and do not know what to do with it. These instances, from widely different periods of history, show that something more than skill is required, something which may perhaps be called "wisdom."

BERTRAND RUSSELL
Unpopular Essays, pp. 21–22

* * *

AN ULTIMATE AIM OF HISTORY

We cannot define the ultimate aim of history but we can posit an aim which is itself a premise for the realization of the highest potentialities. And that is *the unity of mankind.*

KARL JASPERS
Way to Wisdom, p. 106

V

Believing

*. . . man's real values have a subtle but
inevitable way of being communicated, and they
affect the significance of everything he does.
These are the vague intangibles—the
"skyhooks"—which are difficult to verbalize but
easy to sense and tremendously potent in their
influence. They provide a . . . fundamental
structure into which the experiences of
every day are absorbed and given meaning.*

O. H. OHMANN
"Skyhooks"

———————————— ✳ ————————————

Valuing

Visioning

Coaching

Motivating

Team Building

Valuing

THE IMPORTANCE OF VALUES

The human being needs a framework of values, a philosophy of life, a religion or religion-surrogate to live by and understand by, in about the same sense that he or she needs sunlight, calcium, or love.

ABRAHAM MASLOW
Toward a Psychology of Being, p. 206

✳ ✳ ✳

AN INTRINSIC PART OF OUR LIVES

. . . our values are so much an intrinsic part of our lives and behavior that we are often unaware of them — or, at least, we are unable to think about them clearly and articulately. Yet our values, along with other factors, clearly determine our choices, as can be proved by presenting men with equally "reasonable" alternative possibilities and comparing the choices they make. Some will choose one course, others another, and each will feel that his election is *the* rational one.

WILLIAM GUTH and RENATO TAGIURI
"Personal Values and Corporate Strategy"

THE IMPORTANCE OF IDEALISM

It is in the nature of a leader's work that he should be a realist and should recognize the need for action, even when the outcome cannot be foreseen, but also that he should be an idealist and in the broadest sense pursue goals some of which can only be attained in a succeeding generation of leaders. . . . To neglect today for tomorrow surely reflects a treacherous sentimentalism; but to shape the present for the future by the surplus of thought and purpose which we now can muster seems the very expression of the idealism which underlies such social coherence as we presently achieve, and without this idealism we see no worthy meaning in our lives, our institutions, or our culture.

CHESTER BARNARD
Organization and Management, p. 110

✳ ✳ ✳

FIRST PRINCIPLES

Every man should expend his chief thought and attention on his first principles: Are they or are they not rightly laid down? And when he has sifted them, all the rest will follow rightly.

SOCRATES
"Cratylus"
(in Hamilton and Cairns, p. 470)

THE SEARCH FOR MEANING

The majority of people who work don't have to for economic *survival* in the short term. Increasingly, they seek, *in addition* to pay and career opportunities, other kinds of income from their jobs, including work they enjoy, colleagues they like working with, and *meaning*. Far too many generalizations are made about work on the basis of the automobile assembly-line stereotype. For the vast majority, work is a far different and far more fulfilling experience. For people in these new circumstances to be satisfied, it helps enormously if they can see the link between what they do and a higher purpose.

RICHARD PASCALE and ANTHONY ATHOS
The Art of Japanese Management, p. 187

* * *

A KEY FUNCTION OF LEADERS

Let us suppose that we were asked for one all-purpose bit of advice for management, one truth that we were able to distill from the excellent companies research. We might be tempted to reply, "Figure out your value system. Decide what your company *stands for.*" . . . Clarifying the value system and breathing life into it are the greatest contributions a leader can make.

THOMAS PETERS and ROBERT WATERMAN
In Search of Excellence, p. 279, p. 291

BELIEVING

THE FOCAL POINT FOR THE VALUE SYSTEM

The manager serves as the focal point for the organization's value system. Influencers direct their statements of preference to him; he, in turn, assimilates and combines these according to the power of the source, and disseminates information on overall organizational values to subordinates who use it as a guide in decision making. The dissemination of values occurs in terms of specific statements on specific issues, not in terms of global preferences.

HENRY MINTZBERG
The Nature of Managerial Work, p. 97

* * *

THE IBM CREDO

I firmly believe that any organization, in order to survive and achieve success, must have a sound set of beliefs on which it premises all its policies and actions.

Next, I believe that the most important factor in corporate success is faithful adherence to those beliefs.

And finally, I believe that if an organization is to meet the challenges of a changing world, it must be prepared to change everything about itself except those beliefs as it moves through corporate life.

THOMAS WATSON, JR.
(in Pascale and Athos, p. 184)

IBM'S BASIC BELIEFS

- **Respect for the individual.** Respect for the dignity and the rights of each person in the organization.

- **Customer service.** To give the best customer service of any company in the world.

- **Excellence.** The conviction that an organization should pursue all tasks with the objective of accomplishing them in a superior way.

RICHARD PASCALE and ANTHONY ATHOS
The Art of Japanese Management, p. 184

✳ ✳ ✳

TRANSLATING GUIDING BELIEFS INTO REALITY

The test of a healthy culture and company is the translation of the guiding beliefs into a reality that is manifest in the people's daily behavior. As troubled companies have unfortunately or fortunately found out, to state something is not to make it real.

STANLEY DAVIS
Managing Corporate Culture, p. 123

MAKING BELIEFS AND VALUES EXPLICIT

Companies that do not make their beliefs and values explicit do not set up yardsticks by which others can judge them, so it is hard to judge whether they succeed or fail in living up to their beliefs. When the espoused beliefs are very clear, however, any drift away from them is more evident.

STANLEY DAVIS
Managing Corporate Culture, p. 63

✳ ✳ ✳

NEED FOR EXAMINING ONE'S VALUES

How does a manager go about making his values explicit to himself? One thing he can do is examine his behavior from time to time with the question in mind of what values he holds. Here, the approach of comparing and contrasting his behavior with the behavior of others facing similar situations and problems is very helpful. But care must be taken to distinguish variations due to the nature of the information available about the situation and problem from variations that result from different values. The latter is what we are interested in.

WILLIAM GUTH and RENATO TAGIURI
"Personal Values and Corporate Strategy"

MAKING ACTION CONSISTENT WITH WORDS

Management can say as much as it wants in whatever media it chooses that "our employees are our most valuable resource." If it says this from one side of its mouth and then from the other orders a layoff as its first action when the going gets tough, then employees correctly decline to believe the words. If people are not treated well, if they are watched and clearly not trusted, if they are never given any feedback except in the form of haranguing or criticism, then they will believe their experience and ignore the fair words.

ROGER D'APRIX
Communicating for Productivity, p. 8

* * *

ALIGNING CORPORATE SYSTEMS
AND GUIDING BELIEFS

When attempting to change the daily culture of a company, aligning corporate systems and the daily culture is particularly important. Every corporation has a host of systems such as those for planning, control, internal and external communications, management information, managing human resources, and others. Their purpose is to support the corporation's objectives. As part of standard management practice, each system should be checked periodically to see whether it is helping or hindering. One way to check is to *ask whether and how each system supports or undermines the guiding beliefs.*

STANLEY DAVIS
Managing Corporate Culture, p. 84

THINK IN TERMS OF CHANGE

Human though all this may be, managers cannot permit themselves to become victims of habit or tradition, the past or the present. Managers must think constantly in terms of change. They must be consciously seeing to it that things are different and that old customs are replaced by new ones, that new goals make old ones look small, that new ideas make present ones inadequate. ... Life is dynamic; society is dynamic; managers, therefore, must be dynamic if they are to keep pace with the conditions about them.

LAWRENCE APPLEY
The Management Evolution, p. 284

* * *

A STRATEGY FOR LEADERSHIP

Over and over again, the leaders we spoke to told us that they did the same things when they took charge of the organizations — they paid attention to what was going on, they determined what part of the events at hand would be important for the future of the organization, they set a new direction, and they concentrated the attention of everyone in the organization on it.

WARREN BENNIS and BURT NANUS
Leaders, p. 88

VISIONING

THE SPARK OF GENIUS

If there is a spark of genius in the leadership function at all, it must lie in this transcending ability, a kind of magic, to assemble—out of all the variety of images, signals, forecasts, and alternatives—a clearly articulated vision of the future that is at once simple, easily understood, clearly desirable, and energizing.

WARREN BENNIS and BURT NANUS
Leaders, p. 103

* * *

DEVELOPING A MENTAL IMAGE

To choose a direction, a leader must first have developed a mental image of a possible and desirable future state of the organization. This image, which we call a *vision*, may be as vague as a dream or as precise as a goal or mission statement. The critical point is that a vision articulates a view of a realistic, credible, attractive future for the organization, a condition that is better in some important way than what now exists.

WARREN BENNIS and BURT NANUS
Leaders, p. 89

BELIEVING

THREE IMPORTANT LEADERSHIP QUALITIES

Possession of three qualities — the ability to attain a clear mental picture, to create a mental picture above and beyond what others have attained, and the capacity to transfer that to the minds of others — is a very important factor in raising some executives to high levels of achievement and recognition. This is one very important art of management, important to all managers whether they are top managers or executives down the line.

LAWRENCE APPLEY
Management in Action, pp. 188–89

✳ ✳ ✳

A BRIDGE FROM THE PRESENT TO THE FUTURE

A vision is a target that beckons. When John Kennedy set a goal of putting a man on the moon by 1970 or Sanford Weill aimed to make American Express the world's leading investment banking company in five years, they were focusing attention on worthwhile and attainable achievements. Note also that a vision always refers to a *future* state, a condition that does not presently exist and never existed before. With a vision, the leader provides the all-important bridge from the present to the future of the organization.

WARREN BENNIS and BURT NANUS
Leaders, pp. 89–90

VISIONING

THE NEED FOR AN OVERARCHING GOAL

The acceptance of an overarching goal *provides a common vision,* a similar frame of reference for all. If members buy into the same goal, the likelihood is increased that they will act in compatible ways despite strong individual differences. . . . The advantage of using the overarching goal to achieve the commonality, rather than common social background, is that the goal is directly task related. People with diverse viewpoints can strive to achieve the same ends.

DAVID BRADFORD and ALLAN COHEN
Managing for Excellence, p. 109

✳ ✳ ✳

A SHARED VISION PROVIDES
A FRAME OF REFERENCE

A shared vision of the future suggests measures of effectiveness for the organization and for all its parts. It helps individuals distinguish between what's good and what's bad for the organization, and what it's worthwhile to want to achieve. And most important, it makes it possible to distribute decision making widely. People can make difficult decisions without having to appeal to higher levels in the organization each time because they know what end results are desired. Thus, in the very real sense, individual behavior can be shaped, directed, and coordinated by the shared and empowering vision of the future.

WARREN BENNIS and BURT NANUS
Leaders, pp. 91–92

BELIEVING

THE CREATING OF FOCUS

Management of attention through *vision* is the *creating of focus.*
Leaders are the most results-oriented individuals in the world, and
results get attention. Their visions or intentions are compelling
and pull people toward them. Intensity coupled with commitment
is magnetic. And these intense personalities do not have to coerce
people to pay attention; they are so intent on what they are doing that, like a child completely absorbed with creating a sand
castle in a sandbox, they draw others in.

WARREN BENNIS and BURT NANUS
Leaders, p. 28

✱ ✱ ✱

DEVELOPING THE OVERARCHING GOAL

A leader cannot discover a goal, as if it already existed and waited
to be unearthed. Instead, it is more appropriate to think of a goal
as being woven from many strands, including core purpose,
feasibility, challenge, and larger significance. The process is dynamic, playing back and forth among ideas about who needs the
department's services, what is exciting to members and to you,
and what is feasible given the skills and resources likely to
be available.

DAVID BRADFORD and ALLAN COHEN
Managing for Excellence, p. 112

ESTABLISHING COMMON PURPOSE

Establishing common purpose begins with an honest, realistic assessment of what the organization presently is and how it is faring. Next, the executive must provide real leadership in creating a common vision as to what the organization wants to become (its long-term values and goals) and how it plans to get there (its strategies). These long-term goals and supporting strategies operationalize the meaning of common purpose. Without common purpose, all organized activity occurs in a vacuum. Its existence is central to effective management.

EDWARD GIBLAN
"The Road to Managerial Wisdom"

* * *

THE GRETZKY FACTOR

Leaders have what I think of as the Gretzky Factor, a certain "touch." Wayne Gretzky, the best hockey player of his generation, said that it's not as important to know where the puck is now as to know where it will be. Leaders have that sense of where the culture is going to be, where the organization must be if it is to grow. If they don't have it as they start, they do when they arrive.

WARREN BENNIS
On Becoming a Leader, p. 199

BELIEVING

TWO ESSENTIAL TASKS

Establishing an operative overarching goal requires two distinctly different tasks of the leader: to *formulate* an appropriate over-arching goal and to *gain its acceptance* by the members. Each task requires different sets of skills. The first task demands intuitive and analytic ability to sense what would excite subordinates, even though they themselves might not be able to; he second requires inspirational and selling ability. Common o both sets of skills is an ability to think beyond the daily routine, to see a greater ision that ties day-to-day activities to significant future goals.

DAVID BRADFORD and ALLAN COHEN
Managing for Excellence, p. 112

✳ ✳ ✳

OBTAINING "OWNERSHIP" OF THE VISION

The leader may be the one who articulates the vision and gives it legitimacy, who expresses the vision in captivating rhetoric that fires the imagination and emotions of followers, who—through the vision—empowers others to make decisions that get things done. But if the organization is to be successful, the image must grow out of the needs of the entire organization and must be "claimed" or "owned" by all the important actors.

WARREN BENNIS and BURT NANUS
Leaders, p. 109

INCORPORATING THE VISION

A vision of the future is not offered once and for all by the leader and then allowed to fade away. It must be repeated time and again. It must be incorporated in the organization's culture and reinforced through the strategy and decision-making process. It must be constantly evaluated for possible change in the light of new circumstances.

WARREN BENNIS and BURT NANUS
Leaders, pp. 108–09

✳ ✳ ✳

CLARIFYING THE GOALS

It seems very clear to me that in an enterprise, if everybody concerned is absolutely clear about the goals and directives and far purposes of the organization, practically all other questions then become simple technical questions of fitting means to the ends. But it is also true that to the extent that these far goals are confused or conflicting or ambivalent or only partially understood, then all the discussion of techniques and methods and means in the world will be of little use.

ABRAHAM MASLOW
Eupsychian Management, p. 41

THE VALUE OF
AN OVERARCHING GOAL

An overarching goal helps *keep the leader and members focused on the larger issues.* Managers can easily be swamped by the day-to-day minutiae of procedures, rules, deadlines, and other annoyances and lose sight of the department's reasons for existence, but continued reference to the goal guards against tunnel vision. ... Further, the overarching goal is important for its *motivational properties.* When the departmental task is defined in terms of a challenge that has a larger meaning, involvement goes up. Most people need to believe in something that is larger than their day-to-day, often mundane, tasks. They are more likely to become committed to making things happen right if they believe in the significance of the unit's goal.

DAVID BRADFORD and ALLAN COHEN
Managing for Excellence, p. 110

WHY VISION IS CENTRAL
TO LEADERSHIP SUCCESS

When the organization has a clear sense of its purpose, direction, and desired future state and when this image is widely shared, individuals are able to find their own roles both in the organization and in the larger society of which they are a part. This empowers individuals and confers status upon them because they can see themselves as part of a worthwhile enterprise. They gain a sense of importance, as they are transformed from robots blindly following instructions to human beings engaged in a creative and purposeful venture.

WARREN BENNIS and BURT NANUS
Leaders, pp. 90–91

Coaching

THE IDEAL TEACHER

The ideal teacher guides his students but does
not pull them along; he urges them to go forward and does not suppress them; he opens the
way, but does not take them to the place.

CONFUCIUS
Lin Yutang—*The Wisdom of Confucius*

* * *

ON COACHING

To coach is largely to facilitate, which literally means "to make
easy"—not less demanding, less interesting or less intense, but
less discouraging, less bound up with excessive controls and com-
plications. . . . Coaching is the process of enabling others to act,
of building on their strengths. . . . Coaching at its heart involves
caring enough about people to take the time to build a personal
relationship with them. Easy to say, tough to do.

TOM PETERS and NANCY AUSTIN
A Passion for Excellence, p. 326, p. 328

TOWARD LIFELONG LEARNING

The innovative organization requires a learning atmosphere throughout the entire business. It creates and maintains continuous learning. No one is allowed to consider himself "finished" at any time. Learning is a continuing process for all members of the organization.

PETER DRUCKER
Management, p. 799

* * *

A DEVELOPMENTAL ORIENTATION

The transformational leader has a developmental orientation toward followers. He evaluates followers' potential both to perform their present job and to hold future positions of greater responsibility. The leader sets examples and assigns tasks on an individual basis to followers to help significantly alter their abilities and motivations as well as to satisfy immediate organizational needs.

BERNARD BASS
"Leadership: Good, Better, Best"

THE REAL MEASURE
OF EFFECTIVENESS

The real measure of the effectiveness of leadership at all levels is what is actually happening to the individuals directly responsible to that leadership—what changes are really taking place in the climate of the workplace, in the caliber of the people, and in the relationships of supervisor and supervised.

LAWRENCE APPLEY
Management in Action, p. 109

* * *

SUCCESS THROUGH
ACCOMPLISHMENT OF OTHERS

If you want the people below you in your organization to derive genuine satisfaction from the achievement of their subordinates, place great emphasis upon the work that is done under their supervision. . . . Ask for the accomplishments of a manager in terms of the accomplishments of his people. Appraise him on the quality of their work and reward him for what they do. Take the emphasis off personal production, and in all probability, credit will be given where credit is due.

LAWRENCE APPLEY
Management in Action, p. 144

A TOUGH APPROACH

The Manager-as-Developer model is basically a tough approach. It is tough in setting high standards (and holding people to them). It is tough in requiring that the manager hold subordinates' feet to the fire when they may want to avoid the difficult issues. It is tough in pushing for conflicts to be identified and worked through rather than smoothed over. It is tough in requiring that people be confronted (rather than shunted aside, or ignored) when they don't come through. And it is tough in demanding that the manager be willing to be open to confrontation as well.

DAVID BRADFORD and ALLAN COHEN
Managing for Excellence, p. 287

❋ ❋ ❋

ESSENTIAL CONDITIONS FOR LEARNING

Looking at good and poor learning experiences, and *considering any learning situation,* there are three essentials that must be present:

1. New ideas, new skills, or new ways to approaching old ideas and skills.

2. An opportunity to put these innovations into practical action.

3. Feedback as to (a) the results of the actions taken and (b) the relationship between what was done at each step of the way and the end result.

CHARLES KEPNER and BENJAMIN TREGOE
"Developing Decision Makers"

ON GIVING PEOPLE HONEST FEEDBACK

All people have the right to know where they stand. This means your caring enough to let someone know in a timely fashion when performance is off track. It takes self-confidence and skill to lead people to recognize problems, as well as successes, in a constructive way. But as a veteran manager said, "It's downright cruel to allow people to flounder when you can see what's happening and you don't do anything to turn it around. There's no excuse for that kind of insensitivity. None."

TOM PETERS and NANCY AUSTIN
A Passion for Excellence, p. 3

✳ ✳ ✳

A FORWARD-LOOKING APPROACH

The tendency to blame others is a backward-looking approach. The past is beyond control and cannot be altered. Only the present and the future are subject to change, and hence only they can be controlled through decisions. The problem-solving approach, therefore, must incorporate an attitude that accepts the past and takes up the problem of what to do to reach present objectives.

NORMAN MAIER
Problem-Solving Discussions and Conferences, p. 73

EFFECTIVE DELEGATION

Delegation is not a simple "gimmick" used by a leader to get rid of work. It is a leadership strategy—a larger plan to get better resources committed to getting work accomplished, and allowing the development of the subordinates at the same time. Effective delegation is the result of serious planning, clearly understanding what is involved before the delegation takes place, and then following through with one's plan for delegation.

WILLIAM DYER
*Contemporary Issues in Management
and Organization Development*, p. 61

* * *

DELEGATION BY RESULTS EXPECTED

Since authority is intended to furnish managers with a tool for so managing as to gain contributions to enterprise objectives, *authority delegated to an individual manager should be adequate to ensure the ability to accomplish results expected.* Too many managers try to partition and define authority on the basis of the rights to be delegated or withheld, rather than looking first at the goals to be achieved and then determining how much discretion is necessary to achieve them. In no other way can a manager delegate authority in accordance with the responsibility exacted.

KOONTZ, O'DONNELL, and WEIHRICH
Management, p. 425

WILLINGNESS TO LET OTHERS MAKE MISTAKES

Although no responsible manager would sit idly by and let a subordinate make a mistake that might endanger the company or the subordinate's position in the company, continual checking on the subordinate to assure that no mistakes are ever made will make true delegation impossible. As everyone makes mistakes, a subordinate must be allowed to make them, and their cost must be charged to investment in personal development.

KOONTZ, O'DONNELL, and WEIHRICH
Management, p. 430

* * *

NO MISTAKES—NO PROGRESS

More important than any single mistake is the percentage of an individual's total errors as against his successes. We are too easily inclined to generalize from the specific and permit one error to lead us into the belief that the person who committed it is completely inadequate. If, however, that error is weighed against the times he has been right, we may be surprised to discover that the error becomes quite insignificant in comparison with his or her overall performance.

LAWRENCE APPLEY
Management in Action, pp. 39–40

ON BEING AN EFFECTIVE DEVELOPER

The Developer is constantly thinking about how to interact with subordinates in ways that get the immediate problem solved and help them learn how to deal with subsequent difficulties. Whether by questioning, direct teaching, sharing information and experience, giving advice, extracting lessons, giving interpersonal feedback, or just keeping quiet while the subordinate works it out alone, the Developer uses naturally arising interactions to foster learning.

DAVID BRADFORD and ALLAN COHEN
Managing for Excellence, pp. 138–39

* * *

CONDUCTING USEFUL "POST MORTEMS"

When the manager is on the job, practice in problem solving is, of course, inevitable. However, an important source of feedback for improving skills is frequently overlooked. This is the critical examination of mistakes that have occurred in order to understand what happened and why. If such "post mortems" comprise no more than a search for the culprit in order to place the blame, they will provide learning of one kind. If, on the other hand, it is recognized that mistakes are an inevitable occurrence in the trial-and-error process of acquiring problem-solving skills, they can be the source of other and more valuable learning.

DOUGLAS McGREGOR
The Human Side of Enterprise, p. 217

THE FUNCTION OF
PERFORMANCE APPRAISAL

The function of performance appraisal is to teach, not to exhort or admonish. The individual can learn if it can be shown that his actions have been on or off target, especially when the target has been objectively defined. He can see the extent to which his actions have been effective or ineffective and adjust them accordingly.

SAUL GELLERMAN
Management by Motivation, pp. 108–09

✳ ✳ ✳

ESTABLISHING A QUARTERLY REVIEW SYSTEM

If our stockholders had a quarterly review system, why shouldn't our executives? I asked myself. I began to develop the management system I still use today. Over the years, I've regularly asked my key people—and I've had them ask *their* key people, and so on down the line—a few basic questions: "What are your objectives for the next ninety days? What are your plans, your priorities, your hopes? And how do you plan to go about achieving them?" . . . The quarterly review system sounds almost too simple—except that it works.

LEE IACOCCA
Iacocca, p. 47

DEALING WITH THE NONPERFORMER

Nonperformers are often—and perhaps in most cases—not "duds." They are only in the wrong place—the proverbial square peg in the round hole. They belong elsewhere, where what they can do is needed and contributes. It is the manager's job, especially with the young knowledge worker, to think through where a nonperformer might be productive and effective, and to say, "You are in the wrong business—you belong *there.*"

PETER DRUCKER
Management, p. 310

✳ ✳ ✳

LEADERS DEVELOP LEADERS

Indeed the best leaders try to train their followers themselves to become leaders. A second-rate executive will often try to suppress leadership because he fears it may rival his own. But the first-rate executive tries to develop leadership in those under him. The great leader tries to develop power wherever he can among those who work with him, and then he gathers all this power and uses it as the energizing force of a progressive enterprise.

MARY PARKER FOLLETT
Freedom and Coordination, p. 57

Motivating

TAPPING THE UNREALIZED POTENTIAL

Many managers would agree that the effectiveness of their organizations would be at least doubled if they could discover how to tap the unrealized potential present in their human resources.

DOUGLAS McGREGOR
The Human Side of Enterprise, p. 4

* * *

THE LIGHT CREATED BY THE LEADER

I have often thought the saying, "An organization is the lengthened shadow of one man," to be a negative statement. It would be more accurate to say that it is the length to which he can cast his *light*, not his shadow, that determines the greatness of an organization and the quality of its substance. The top leader should cast no shade — shade that obscures the contributions of other people — shade in which freedom of thought and action cannot grow and flourish. Rather he should create light which draws all the energies and creativity of *many* minds toward the objective that the organization has set up as its goal.

LAWRENCE APPLEY
Management in Action, pp. 114–15

ON BEING
AN EFFECTIVE MOTIVATOR

I've always felt that a manager has achieved a great deal when he's able to motivate one other person. When it comes to making the place run, motivation is everything. You might be able to do the work of two people, but you can't *be* two people. Instead, you have to inspire the next guy down the line and get him to inspire *his* people.

LEE IACOCCA
Iacocca, p. 9

✳ ✳ ✳

THE JACKASS FALLACY

Frequently, I have asked executives this question: What is the dominant philosophy of motivation in American management? Almost invariably, they quickly agree that it is the carrot-and-stick philosophy, reward and punishment. Then I ask them to close their eyes for a moment, and to form a picture in their mind's eye with a carrot at one end and a stick at the other. When they have done so, I then ask them to describe the central image in that picture. Most frequently they respond that the central figure is a jackass.

HARRY LEVINSON
"Asinine Attitudes Toward Motivation"

A SELF-FULFILLING PROPHECY

The characteristics of a jackass are stubbornness, stupidity, willfulness, and unwillingness to go where someone is driving him. These, by interesting coincidence, are also characteristics of the unmotivated employee. Thus it becomes vividly clear that the underlying assumption which managers make about motivation leads to a self-fulfilling prophecy. People inevitably respond to the carrot-and-stick by trying to get more of the carrot while protecting themselves against the stick.

HARRY LEVINSON
"Asinine Attitudes Toward Motivation"

* * *

THE RESPONSE OF THE
COG IN THE MACHINE

And now I would ask the question, "How can any human being help but be insulted by being treated as an interchangeable part, as simply a cog in a machine, as no more than an appurtenance to an assembly line?" There *is* no other human, reasonable, intelligible way to respond to this kind of profound cutting off of half of one's growth possibilities than by getting angry or resentful or struggling to get out of the situation.

ABRAHAM MASLOW
Eupsychian Management, pp. 46–47

THE FUTILITY OF THE GUN

An organization fostering a more human environment is likely to be more productive and more effective than an organization which treats human values lightly. I take issue with my acquaintance who asserted that performance in the real world is more a matter of holding a gun to people's heads than it is anything else. I believe that the gun only makes people so nervous and preoccupied that their performance is riddled with fear and self-doubt. I have yet to see people give generously of their talents when they were living under the gun.

ROGER D'APRIX
Communicating for Productivity, p. 94

* * *

MOTIVATING VS. MOVING

The reward is the personal satisfaction in what you do. What management has failed to do—incredibly failed to do—is capitalize on the human desire for achievement. Managements have always looked at man as an animal to be manipulated with a carrot and a stick. They found that when man hurts, he will move to avoid pain—and they say, "We're motivating the employees." Hell, you're not motivating them, you're moving them. . . . Another and far more efficient way of getting people to do a good job is to give them the opportunity to get satisfaction out of doing a good job.

FREDERICK HERZBERG
Dowling—*Effective Management*
& the Behavioral Sciences, p. 44

THE ESSENTIAL SKILL

The nature of leadership skills will vary with the situation, but one talent all leaders must possess — the capacity to perceive needs of followers in relationship to their own, to help followers move toward fuller self-realization and self-actualization along with the leaders themselves.

JAMES MacGREGOR BURNS
Leadership, p. 116

✳ ✳ ✳

UNDERSTANDING HUMAN NEEDS

Leaders must understand the needs of the people they work with — their needs at the most basic level for income, jobs, housing and health care; their need for a measure of security; their need for confidence in the stability of the system of which they are a part; their need for a sense of community, of identity and belonging, of mutual trust, of loyalty to one another; their need for recognition, for the respect of others, for reassurance that they as individuals are needed; their need for new challenges and a conviction that their competencies are being well used.

JOHN GARDNER
On Leadership, p. 185

MOTIVATING

UNEXPRESSED NEEDS

The most gifted leaders understand that the needs of people cannot be fully plumbed by asking them what they want or why they want it. One of the deepest of truths about the cry of the human heart is that it is so often muted, so often a cry that is never uttered. ... We die with much unsaid. It is strange that members of a species renowned for communicative gifts should leave unexpressed some of their deepest yearnings, their smoldering resentments, their worries and secret hopes, their longing to serve a higher purpose.

JOHN GARDNER
On Leadership, p. 186

* * *

EMPOWERMENT

Leaders *empower others to translate intention into reality and sustain it.* This does not mean that leaders must relinquish power, or that followers must continually challenge authority. It does mean that power must become a unit of exchange — an active, changing token in creative, productive, and communicative transactions. Effective leaders will ultimately reap the human harvest of their efforts by the simple action of power's reciprocal: *empowerment.*

WARREN BENNIS and BURT NANUS
Leaders, p. 80

TREATING PEOPLE WITH DIGNITY

I think that this kind of psychodynamic understanding of self-esteem and of dignity would make a great difference in the industrial situation because the feeling of dignity, of respect and of self-respect are *so easy to give*! It costs little or nothing; it's a matter of an attitude, a deep-lying sympathy and understanding which can express itself almost automatically in various ways that can be quite satisfying.

ABRAHAM MASLOW
Eupsychian Management, p. 48

* * *

PULLING RATHER THAN PUSHING

The essential thing in organizational leadership is that the leader's style *pulls* rather than *pushes* people on. A pull style of influence works by attracting and energizing people to an exciting vision of the future. It motivates by identification, rather than through rewards and punishments. The leaders in our study articulate and embody the ideals toward which the organization is striving. They enroll themselves (and others) in a vision of that ideal as attainable and worthy.

WARREN BENNIS and BURT NANUS
Leaders, p. 80

UNDERSTANDING THE OTHER'S VIEWS

The behavioral researcher starts with a premise that is easy enough to test: that everyone's behavior is reasonably logical and justifiable *to himself.* To understand another person's actions, you must see his situation the way he sees it. This does not necessarily mean agreeing with him; it means trying to discover his basic premises. Whether he or anyone else is "right" or "wrong" in the way he views his world is quite irrelevant. What matters is what he believes, because that determines how he behaves.

SAUL GELLERMAN
Management by Motivation, p. 17

* * *

THE ULTIMATE MOTIVATION

The ultimate motivation of any individual is to make the self-concept real: to live in a manner that is appropriate to one's preferred role, to be treated in a manner that corresponds to one's preferred rank, and to be rewarded in a manner that reflects one's estimate of his own abilities.

SAUL GELLERMAN
Motivation and Productivity, p. 290

CONFIRMING ONE'S POTENTIALITY

I meet another—I accept and confirm him as he now is. But confirming a person *as he is* is only the first step, for confirmation does not mean that I take his appearance at this moment as the person I want to confirm. I must take the other person in his dynamic existence, in his specific potentiality. How can I confirm what I want most to confirm in his present being? That is the hidden, for in the present lies hidden what *can become.* His potentiality makes itself felt to me as that which I would most confirm.

MARTIN BUBER
A *Believing Humanism,* pp. 170–71

✳ ✳ ✳

RELATING WORK TO WORTHWHILE ENDS

The effective leader is able to help people in the organization know pride and satisfaction in their work. Great leaders often inspire their followers to high levels of achievement by showing them how their work contributes to worthwhile ends. It is an emotional appeal to some of the most fundamental of human needs— the need to be important, to make a difference, to feel useful, to be a part of a successful and worthwhile enterprise.

WARREN BENNIS and BURT NANUS
Leaders, pp. 92–93

THE THREE STONECUTTERS

An old story tells of three stonecutters who were asked what they were doing. The first replied, "I am making a living." The second kept on hammering while he said, "I am doing the best job of stonecutting in the entire country." The third one looked up with a visionary gleam in his eyes and said, "I am building a cathedral."

PETER DRUCKER
Management, p. 431

* * *

A SYNERGISTIC RELATION

The highest point of self-motivation arises when there is a complementary conjunction of the individual's needs and the organization's requirements. The requirements of both mesh, interrelate, and become synergistic. The energies of the individual and the organization are pooled for mutual advantage.

HARRY LEVINSON
"Management by Whose Objectives?"

* * *

INFECTIOUS OPTIMISM

The leader must have infectious optimism. . . . The final test of a leader is the feeling you have when you leave his presence after a conference. Have you a feeling of uplift and confidence?

FIELD MARSHAL BERNARD MONTGOMERY
(in Peters and Austin, p. 264)

THE USE OF POSITIVE REINFORCEMENT

It is easier to build up a specific connection between a reward and a desired behavior than between a penalty and a proscribed behavior. If individuals are traumatized they may become ego defensive and fail to learn what it is they should not do. Positive reinforcement, as experiments demonstrate, is a more reliable and easier technique to administer than negative reinforcement. It is also less subject to undesirable side effects.

DANIEL KATZ and ROBERT KAHN
The Social Psychology of Organizations, p. 310

* * *

SHOWING CONCERN

What can managers do that will show another person that the manager is truly concerned about him or her as a person? (1) talk with people—which means asking, listening, and sharing; (2) trust people with significant work; (3) allow people to influence their work world; (4) reward people for good work; (5) help people plan a future; and (6) take time to "coach" people.

WILLIAM DYER
*Contemporary Issues in Management
and Organization Development*, pp. 74–75

ENCOURAGING INDIVIDUAL CONTRIBUTIONS

In corporate life, you have to encourage all your people to make a contribution to the common good and to come up with better ways of doing things. You don't have to accept every single suggestion, but if you don't get back to the guy and say, "Hey, that idea was terrific," and pat him on the back, he'll never give you another one. That kind of communication lets people know they really count.

LEE IACOCCA
Iacocca, p. 54

✳ ✳ ✳

RECOGNIZING DIVERSITY

The simple act of recognizing diversity in corporate life helps us to connect the great variety of gifts that people bring to the work and service of the organization. Diversity allows each of us to contribute in a special way, to make our special gift a part of the corporate effort.

MAX DePREE
Leadership is an Art, p. 7

MOVING BEYOND CHECKERS AND CHESS

To move from manipulation to power-wielding is to move from checkers to chess. But democratic leadership moves far beyond chess because, as we play the game, the chessmen come alive. The bishops and knights and pawns take part on their own terms and with their own motivations, values, and goals, and the game moves ahead with new momentum, direction, and possibilities. In real life the most practical advice for leaders is not to treat pawns like pawns, nor princes like princes, but all persons like *persons*.

JAMES MacGREGOR BURNS
Leadership, pp. 461–62

* * *

THE CHALLENGE FOR EVERY MANAGER

It is clear that the task of creating a more highly motivated workforce is complex. It is *not* something that can be done with poster displays, campaigns, and across-the-board programs. It is a long-term process. It requires not only tremendous effort, but imagination and deep commitment. Motivating workers is not a special assignment for a group of specialists; it is an integral part of every manager's job.

DELMAR LANDEN and HOWARD CARLSON
"New Strategies for Motivating Employees"
(in Marrow, *The Failure of Success*)

ON CREATING A LEGACY

To the extent that leaders enable followers to develop their own initiative, they are creating something that can survive their own departure. Some individuals who have dazzling powers of personal leadership create dependency in those below them and leave behind a weakened organization staffed by weakened people. Leaders who strengthen their people may create a legacy that will last for a very long time.

JOHN GARDNER
On Leadership, p. 36

Team Building

THE ROOTS OF PARTICIPATIVE MANAGEMENT

Around 100 A.D., a Roman landowner wrote of his approach to managing the workers of his estate:

> Nowadays I make it a practice to call them into consultation on any new work. . . . I observe that they are more willing to set about a piece of work on which their opinions have been asked and their advice followed.

> COLUMELLA
> *On Agriculture I*
> (in Sashkin, p. 10)

✻ ✻ ✻

THE MOST IMPORTANT THING

Not long ago a young man asked me, "What is the most important thing to have in mind if I think I have it in me to lead?" I said, "The most important thing to have in mind is that leaders need followers." I was not being flippant.

> JOHN GARDNER
> *On Leadership*, p. 166

TEAM BUILDING

THE CHANGING ROLE OF THE MANAGER

The role of the manager has changed significantly in many organizations. The strong manager capable of almost single-handedly turning around an organization or department, while still a folk hero in the eyes of many, has given way to the recent demands of increasingly complex systems for managers who are able to pull together people of diverse backgrounds, personalities, training, and experience and weld them into an effective working group.

WILLIAM DYER
Team Building, p. xi

* * *

THE HEROIC MANAGER

When American managers talk about their vision of managing — the idealized models of their imagination — the same few cultural heroes glorified in film and fiction are frequently mentioned. Heroic managers secretly view themselves as direct descendents of the frontiersman, that quiet but tough adventurer who was constantly setting out for new territory, long an ideal in American literature, film, mythology, and consciousness. The Lone Ranger, an imposing masked figure, rides up on a white horse to overcome great odds in solving the problem of the day. This model of the vanquishing leader — a bit mysterious, generous but aloof — is a very common theme.

DAVID BRADFORD and ALLAN COHEN
Managing for Excellence, p. 26

THE FRUSTRATING TRAP FOR THE HEROIC MANAGER

The most paradoxical and frustrating trap for the heroic manager is that greater effort exacerbates the problem. While increasingly Herculean efforts are demanded of the leader, the abilities of subordinates are further ignored, causing frustration and weakening of motivation throughout the organization. Heroism sets up a self-defeating cycle: The more the manager accepts the responsibility for departmental success, the greater the likelihood that subordinates will yield it, forcing the manager to take more, and so on. The manager is driven to get more involved — to be as central to the department as a nerve center or orchestra conductor — desperately trying to control all the diverse parts of the organization, but still unable to produce excellence.

DAVID BRADFORD and ALLAN COHEN
Managing for Excellence, p. 17

* * *

THE MANAGER AS TEAM BUILDER

The modern manager has shifted from dealing with problems on a one-to-one basis to solving more problems collectively, involving everyone who has a contribution to make in either solving a problem or implementing actions. In this context, the manager is a coach, a facilitator, a developer, a team builder.

WILLIAM DYER
Team Building, p. xi

TEAM BUILDING

ON SHARING THE MANAGEMENT RESPONSIBILITY

To achieve excellence in earthly organizations, a manager must first believe in the concept and then act in the creation of a team of key subordinates who are jointly responsible with the manager for the department's success. At the same time that the manager works to develop management responsibility in subordinates, he or she must help develop the subordinates' abilities to share management of the unit's performance.

DAVID BRADFORD and ALLAN COHEN
Managing for Excellence, pp. 60–61

❊ ❊ ❊

ABILITY TO ORGANIZE
ALL THE FORCES

The leader is one who can organize the experience of the group—can organize the experience of the group and thus get the full power of the group. The leader makes the team. This is preeminently the leadership quality—the ability to organize all the forces there are in an enterprise and make them serve a common purpose.

MARY PARKER FOLLETT
Freedom and Coordination, p. 52

BUILDING THE TEAM

Teams are collections of people who must rely on group collaboration if each member is to experience the optimum of success and goal achievement. It is obvious that in order to score touchdowns (and prevent the opponent from scoring) a football team has to play together. It should be just as obvious that a work unit or a management group must also work together to ensure success.

WILLIAM DYER
Team Building, p. 4

✳ ✳ ✳

COMPLEMENTARY SKILLS

Team leadership enhances the possibility that different styles of leadership—and different skills—can be brought to bear simultaneously. If the leader is a visionary with little talent for practical steps, a team member who is a naturally gifted agenda setter can provide priceless support. The important thing is not that the leader cover all bases but that the team collectively do so. The best leader is one who ensures that the appropriate talent and skill are built into the team.

JOHN GARDNER
On Leadership, p. 150

CHARACTERISTICS OF THE EFFECTIVE TEAM

The effective team has these characteristics: (1) there is a climate of trust and support; (2) an ability to communicate and share information about significant matters is in evidence; (3) goals and decisions are understood and accepted; (4) people feel they can influence what happens; (5) leadership is not restrictive, punitive, or highly authoritarian; and (6) people accept and implement assignments and decisions.

WILLIAM DYER
*Contemporary Issues in Management
and Organization Development*, pp. 214–15

* * *

ACHIEVING A REALIZATION OF BELONGINGNESS

One of the most effective ways to give people a realization of "belongingness" is to ask them to help you as their leader: take an inventory of where the group is; determine where the group should go; determine who and what is needed to get the group there; determine how well individuals in the group should perform; determine how well they are performing; determine what is needed to help them perform better; and determine how they should share in the outcome. This works! I know it works! But let me remind you it takes a deep belief in human values and skill in conducting group discussions.

LAWRENCE APPLEY
Formula for Success, p. 45

INVOLVEMENT IN GROUP GOALS

Teamwork requires an understanding of, and commitment to, the group goals. Whether a regular work group, a project team, or a special task force, the need for the group to determine and understand its goals will be a prerequisite for effective team building. . . . The members of the group, to achieve teamwork, will need to not only understand these goals but have a degree of commitment to them so as to work effectively toward their achievement.

GORDON LIPPITT
Organization Renewal, p. 107

✱ ✱ ✱

PARTICIPATION IN DECISION MAKING

I don't set goals for other people. That is one of their key jobs — to define their goals, to define success. I set goals for myself, but not for other people. I set the company goals in my own mind, and then they come out in discussions. But I don't sort of lay them down . . . I've never taken a major decision without consulting my colleagues. It would be unimaginable to me, unimaginable. First, they help me make a better decision in most cases. Second, if they know about it and agree with it, they'll back it. Otherwise, they might challenge it, not openly, but subconsciously . . .

SIR ALASTAIR PILKINGTON
Chairman, Pilkington Brothers, Ltd.
(in Quinn, p. 65)

TEAM BUILDING

THE PROMOTION OF HONEST FEEDBACK

Honest, sincere feedback between all the members of a team (including the leader) is one of the foundations on which mutual trust is built. It is in this sense that open communication and trust are reciprocal. ... Genuine feedback of this kind *identifies a problem that can be explored* and probably solved.

DOUGLAS McGREGOR
The Professional Manager, pp. 175–76

✳ ✳ ✳

CONSTRUCTIVE USE OF CONFLICT

Conflict and differences of opinion always exist in a healthy, virile organization, for it is usually from such differences that new and better objectives and methods emerge. Differences are essential to progress, but bitter, unresolved differences can immobilize an organization. The central problem, consequently, becomes not how to reduce or eliminate conflict, but how to deal constructively with it. Effective organizations have extraordinary capacity to handle conflict.

RENSIS LIKERT
New Patterns of Management, p. 117

A WIN-WIN APPROACH TO CONFLICT RESOLUTION

Suppose two people want an orange and only one is available. Each feels he should have the orange. Once the conflict is established, a compromise seems the only alternative. Each person could have half an orange. But if the problem is probed to discover why each wants the orange, it may be that one wants the juice and the other wants the skin. In this situation, each can achieve his full goal.

NORMAN R.F. MAIER
The Appraisal Interview, p. 200

＊ ＊ ＊

ORGANIZING DISSENT

Effective decision makers organize dissent. This protects them against being taken in by the plausible but false or incomplete. It gives them the alternatives so that they can choose and make a decision, but also ensures that they are not lost in the fog when their decision proves deficient or wrong in execution. And it forces the imagination—their own and that of their associates. Dissent converts the plausible into the right and the right into the good decision.

PETER DRUCKER
Management, p. 474

HOW DO I KNOW I AM RIGHT?

There are few if any ways to determine previously the rightness or wrongness of certain courses of action. There is, however, a helpful principle. He who seeks the advice and counsel of others will be more right than if he did not. After one has reviewed various courses of action with those who can be helpful, he at least can rest in the realization that he has reached a conclusion that is as right as could be arrived at under the conditions.

LAWRENCE APPLEY
Values in Management, pp. 242–43

✳ ✳ ✳

CONFORMITY TO GROUP NORMS

In studies of social clubs and other small groups, conformity pressures have frequently been observed. Whenever a member says something that sounds out of line with the group's norms, the members at first increase their communication with the deviant. Attempts to influence the nonconformist member to revise or tone down his dissident ideas continue as long as most members of the group feel hopeful about talking him into changing his mind. But if they fail after repeated attempts, the amount of communication they direct toward the deviant decreases markedly. The members begin to exclude him, often quite subtly at first and later more obviously, in order to restore the unity of the group.

IRVING JANIS
Groupthink, p. 5

BEWARE OF GROUPTHINK

I use the term "groupthink" as a quick and easy way to refer to a mode of thinking that people engage in when they are deeply involved in a cohesive ingroup, when the members' striving for unanimity overrides their motivation to realistically appraise alternative courses of action. "Groupthink" is a term of the same order as the words in the newspeak vocabulary George Orwell presents in his dismaying *1984*—a vocabulary with terms such as "double-think" and "crimethink." By putting groupthink with those Orwellian words, I realize that groupthink takes on an invidious connotation. The invidiousness is intentional: groupthink refers to a deterioration of mental efficiency, reality testing, and moral judgment that results from ingroup pressures.

IRVING JANIS
Groupthink, p. 9

WATERGATE GROUPTHINK

In the early days of that modern morality play called the Watergate hearings, there was a moment of striking relevance when Senator Howard Baker of Tennessee was questioning Herbert Porter, the thirty-five-year-old staff man who had passed large sums in cash to Watergate conspirator Gordon Liddy to use in the "dirty tricks" part of the reelection campaign.

"Why?" the Senator asked. "Where does the system break down, when a person . . . abdicates his conscience? . . . Did you ever have qualms about what you were doing?"

"I think the thought crossed my head, Senator," the witness replied, "in all honesty, that I really could not see what effect it had on reelecting a president of the United States. On the other hand, in all fairness, I was not the one to stand up in a meeting and say that this should be stopped. I kind of drifted along."

HARLAN CLEVELAND
The Knowledge Executive, p. 159–60

✳ ✳ ✳

THE PROBLEM WITH GROUPTHINK

The central theme of my analysis (of groupthink) can be summarized in this generalization: The more amiability and esprit de corps among the members of a policy-making ingroup, the greater is the danger that independent critical thinking will be replaced by groupthink, which is likely to result in irrational and dehumanizing actions directed against outgroups.

IRVING JANIS
Groupthink, p. 13

BELIEVING

PREVENTING GROUPTHINK

The leader of a policy-forming group should assign the role of critical evaluator to each member, encouraging the group to give high priority to airing objections and doubts. This practice needs to be reinforced by the leader's acceptance of criticism of his or her own judgments in order to discourage the members from soft-pedaling their disagreements.

If the proposed practice is wholeheartedly approved and reinforced by the chief executive and the other top executives in the organization's hierarchy, it might help to counteract the spontaneous group pressures that give rise to a premature consensus.

IRVING JANIS
Groupthink, p. 262

* * *

THE VALUE OF PARTICIPATION

A great deal of research has shown that a major way of changing the work environment is to increase the participation of people in planning, goal-setting, and decision-making processes. There has been clear research evidence that the motivational forces for many people are stimulated when they are involved in determining the cause of their own actions. . . . When there is honest involvement—people being asked for their ideas and suggestions and these ideas being listened to and utilized—participation has been noted time after time to result in improved performance.

WILLIAM DYER
*Contemporary Issues in Management
and Organization Development*, p. 66

VI

Being

*At every moment you choose yourself. But do
you choose your self? Body and soul contain a
thousand possibilities out of which you can
build many I's. But in only one of them is
there a congruence of the elector and the elected.*

DAG HAMMARSKJÖLD
Markings, p. 17

━━━━━━━━━━━━━━━━━━ ✳ ━━━━━━━━━━━━━━━━━━

Identity

Independence

Authenticity

Responsibility

Courage

Identity

A FIRM SENSE OF IDENTITY

The exercise of leadership requires a strong sense of identity—knowing who one is and who one is not. The myth of the value of being an "all-around guy" is damaging to the striving of an individual to locate himself from within and then to place himself in relation to others. This active location and placement of one's self prevents the individual from being defined by others in uncongenial terms. It prevents him also from being buffeted around the sea of opinions he must live within. A sense of autonomy, separateness, or identity permits a freedom of action and thinking so necessary for leadership.

ABRAHAM ZALEZNIK
"The Human Dilemmas of Leadership"

* * *

THE KEY PROBLEM TO IDENTITY

The key problem of identity is (as the term connotes) the capacity of the ego to sustain sameness and continuity in the face of changing fate. But fate always combines changes in inner conditions, which are the result of ongoing life stages, and changes in the milieu, the historical situation. Identity connotes the resiliency of maintaining essential patterns in the processes of change. Thus, strange as it may seem, it takes a well-established identity to tolerate radical change, for the well-established identity has arranged itself around basic values which cultures have in common.

ERIK ERIKSON
Insight and Responsibility, pp. 95–96

BEING

THE BASIC QUESTION

It seems to me that at bottom each person is asking, "Who am I, *really?* How can I get in touch with this real self, underlying all my surface behavior? How can I become myself?"

CARL ROGERS
On Becoming a Person, p. 108

* * *

A DEFINITION

Identity is the experience which permits a person to say legitimately "I"—"I" as an organizing active center of the structure of all my actual or potential activities.

ERICH FROMM
The Revolution of Hope, pp. 82–83

* * *

A COHERENT SENSE OF SELF

Identity is a coherent sense of self. It depends upon the awareness that one's endeavors and one's life make sense, that they are meaningful in the context in which life is lived. It depends also upon stable values, and upon the conviction that one's actions and values are harmoniously related. It is a sense of wholeness, of integration, of knowing what is right and what is wrong and of being able to choose.

ALLEN WHEELIS
The Quest for Identity, p. 19

CONSISTENCY OF SELF

A self must have some consistency; its actions tomorrow must be recognizably of a piece with the actions which it carried out yesterday.

JACOB BRONOWSKI
The Identity of Man, p. 15

✳ ✳ ✳

FAITH IN THE PERSISTENCE OF SELF

Unless we have faith in the persistence of our self, our feeling of identity is threatened and we become dependent on other people whose approval then becomes the basis for our feeling of identity.

ERICH FROMM
The Art of Loving, p. 123

✳ ✳ ✳

THE SELF AS THE CENTER

The self is thus not merely the sum of the various "roles" one plays — it is the capacity by which one *knows* he plays these roles; it is the center from which one sees and is aware of these so-called different "sides" of himself.

ROLLO MAY
Man's Search for Himself, p. 92

BEING

A UNIFIED PERSONALITY

Personality characteristics vary according to the *degree of unity* or the amount of scatter in the meaningful elements in a given individual. The more scattered and disconnected these elements are the more abnormal the individual. Alternatively we observe that everything meaningful in the given unity achieves a certain *equilibrium and harmony* which together form a whole.

KARL JASPERS
General Psychopathology, p. 439

✳ ✳ ✳

IDENTITY AND VALUES

Identity is founded on value. It is founded, specifically, on those values which are at the top of the hierarchy—the beliefs, faiths, and ideals which integrate and determine subordinate values.

ALLEN WHEELIS
The Quest for Identity, p. 200

✳ ✳ ✳

HAVING A HIERARCHY OF VALUES

Only in the compelling moments of decision, not in mere cogitation, is it revealed what has priority for a man, whether his life is determined by a hierarchy of values or is a mere succession of contradictory states without any meaning.

KARL JASPERS
Philosophy is for Everyman, p. 63

CREATING YOUR OWN IDENTITY

Modern man cannot recapture an identity out of the past; for his old identity was not lost, but outgrown. Identity is not, therefore, to be found; it is to be created and achieved.

ALLEN WHEELIS
The Quest for Identity, p. 205

✳ ✳ ✳

A PHILOSOPHY OF LIFE

A self-acquired and tested philosophy of life is ultimately related to the individual's mental health. For it has the capacity to project meaning into confusion, frustration, and anxiety, and to maintain stability throughout change. The framework and perspective that it provides go a long way toward avoiding the shaky, fragmented mentality of him who knows the price of everything and the value of nothing, or has everything to live with and nothing to live for.

E. MARIAN KINGET
On Being Human, p. 194

✳ ✳ ✳

A COMPASS AND BALLAST

A firm sense of identity provides both a compass to determine one's course in life and ballast to keep one steady. So equipped and provisioned, one can safely ignore much of the buffeting. Without such protection more vigilance is needed; each vicissitude, inner and outer, must be defined and watched.

ALLEN WHEELIS
The Quest for Identity, pp. 21–22

Independence

ON REMAINING IMMATURE

Through laziness and cowardice a large part of mankind, even after nature has freed them from alien guidance, gladly remain immature. It is because of laziness and cowardice that it is so easy for others to usurp the role of guardians. It is so comfortable to be a minor! If I have a book which provides meaning for me, a pastor who has a conscience for me, a doctor who will judge my diet for me, and so forth, I need not exert myself. I do not have any need to think; if I can only pay, others will take over the tedious job for me.

IMMANUEL KANT
On History, p. 3

* * *

ON QUESTIONING TRADITION

Certainly there is risk in deviating from the wisdom embodied in concrete tradition. But there is also risk in accepting a tradition without questioning it.

PAUL TILLICH
Morality and Beyond, pp. 44–45

LACK OF SELFHOOD

Often he (the client) discovers that he exists only in response to the demands of others, that he seems to have no self of his own, that he is only trying to think, and feel, and behave in the way that others believe he *ought* to think, and feel and behave.

CARL ROGERS
On Becoming a Person, p. 110

* * *

LIVING FROM THE IMAGE

Many individuals are determined in their inner focus by how they appear to others, that they all refer back to the image that they produce in others. They do not live from the core out, not to the other from their own center, but from the image that they produce in others.

MARTIN BUBER
A Believing Humanism, p. 149

* * *

FOR BETTER FOR WORSE

There is a time in every man's education when he arrives at the conviction that envy is ignorance; that imitation is suicide; that he must take himself for better for worse as his portion; that though the wide universe is full of good, no kernel of nourishing corn can come to him but through his toil bestowed on that plot of ground which is given him to till.

RALPH WALDO EMERSON
"Self-Reliance," in *Emerson's Essays*, p. 32

PERSONAL STYLE

A personal style is a way of achieving definiteness and effectiveness in our self-image and in our relationships with other people. Style is the stamp of individuality impressed upon our adaptive behavior. It evolves gradually by our adopting a consistent line of procedure and sticking to it.

GORDON ALLPORT
Becoming, p. 78

✳ ✳ ✳

THE INNER-DIRECTED PERSON

The inner-directed person becomes capable of maintaining a delicate balance between the demands upon him of his life goal and the buffetings of his external environment.

DAVID RIESMAN
The Lonely Crowd, p. 16

✳ ✳ ✳

HAVING THOUGHTS OF YOUR OWN

The right to express our thoughts means something only if we are able to have thoughts of our own; freedom from external authority is a lasting gain only if the inner psychological conditions are such that we are able to establish our own individuality.

ERICH FROMM
Escape from Freedom, p. 241

THE PERSON WHO PHILOSOPHIZES

But every man who philosophizes is himself and cannot simply choose the philosophy of another. He will adopt it, will convert it into a being of his own, will be awakened and illuminated by the other who speaks to him in a philosophical work—but he will maintain his testing, questioning posture.

KARL JASPERS
Philosophy I, p. 299

* * *

CHOOSING YOUR OWN PLAN

He who lets the world, or his own portion of it, choose his plan of life for him has no need of any other faculty than the ape-like one of imitation. He who chooses his plan for himself employs all his faculties.

JOHN STUART MILL
On Liberty, p. 71

INDEPENDENCE WITHIN THE GROUP

The individual must be able to belong to his group with passionately active and passionately combative love. At the same time, however, he must refuse to let the power of any slogan coined within the group prevent him from standing up for what is right, for worthy and adequate rather than unworthy and inadequate means.

MARTIN BUBER
Israel and the World, p. 47

* * *

THE VALUE OF INDIVIDUALITY

In proportion to the development of his individuality, each person becomes more valuable to himself, and is, therefore, capable of being more valuable to others. There is greater fullness of life about his own existence, and when there is more life in the units there is more in the mass which is composed of them.

JOHN STUART MILL
On Liberty, p. 76

Authenticity

BEING YOURSELF

Rabbi Zusya said, a short while before his death: "In the world to come I shall not be asked: 'Why were you not Moses?' I shall be asked: 'Why were you not Zusya?'"

MARTIN BUBER
The Way of Man, p. 17

* * *

THE PROBLEM

A man who has a beautiful soul always has some beautiful things to say, but a man who says beautiful things does not necessarily have a beautiful soul.

CONFUCIUS
Lin Yutang—*The Wisdom of Confucius*, pp. 179–80

ON BEING ENCASED

Each of us is encased in an armour which we soon, out of familiarity, no longer notice.

MARTIN BUBER
Between Man and Man, p. 10

* * *

THE AUTOMATON

Giving up spontaneity and individuality results in a thwarting of life. Psychologically the automaton, while being alive biologically, is dead emotionally and mentally. While he goes through the motions of living, his life runs through his hands like sand.

ERICH FROMM
Escape from Freedom, p. 255

* * *

ON ACTING A PART

I see at once how false to myself my habitual way of life has been, even when I thought I was being sincere. I realize that I have been acting a part, a personage very different from what I really am. Thus, laid bare, I find myself again, and at once I experience a tremendous urge to assert myself as I am.

PAUL TOURNIER
The Meaning of Persons, p. 22

THE ORIGIN OF CONFLICT

The origin of all conflict between me and my fellow men is that I do not say what I mean, and that I do not do what I say.

MARTIN BUBER
Hasidism and Modern Man, p. 158

❋ ❋ ❋

A DEFINITION

Authenticity is the reduction of phoniness toward the zero point.

ABRAHAM MASLOW
The Farther Reaches of Human Nature, p. 183

❋ ❋ ❋

THE WONDER OF WONDERS

The wonder of wonders, the one and only true being I can meet, is the man who is himself. He will not rigidly cling to anything that he has objectified as valid; he permits and asks limitless questions, not at random, but so that his self will speak and reply.

KARL JASPERS
Philosophy II, p. 41

ON BEING SINCERE

When we say a man is sincere we mean basically that he says what he thinks — that is, his thoughts and speech are identical and form a complete unity. This does not mean he utters the objective truth. Objective truth is not granted to mortals. But he says what he thinks. His mouth speaks what he thinks.

MARTIN BUBER
(in Hodes — *Martin Buber,* p. 65)

* * *

THE ESSENCE OF HONESTY

In its most basic form, honesty has to do with one's own self, one's own feelings, perceptions, moment-to-moment experiencing. It is the direct communication of the actuality of one's being. In honesty, one does not explain or interpret the feelings of others but refers solely to one's own experiencing.

CLARK MOUSTAKAS
Loneliness and Love, p. 118

* * *

REVEALING YOUR TRUE BEING

When a person is authentic he not only acknowledges the truth of his feelings, needs, and wishes, but he is capable of revealing his true being to the other people with whom he has personal relationships.

SIDNEY JOURARD
Healthy Personality, p. 168

AUTHENTICITY

PROVIDING THE KEY

If a man chooses to be fully known, he will show himself freely to another man, in all possible ways. His behavior, which is the "outside" of his being-for-himself (his experience), is unintelligible, however, unless he provides the observer with the key.

SIDNEY JOURARD
Disclosing Man to Himself, p. 19

* * *

SAYING WHAT YOU THINK AND FEEL

Whether or not we are aware of it, there is nothing of which we are more ashamed than of not being ourselves, and there is nothing that gives us greater pride than to think, to feel, and to say what is ours.

ERICH FROMM
Escape from Freedom, p. 262

* * *

SOUND ADVICE

Never, "for the sake of peace and quiet," deny your own experience and convictions.

DAG HAMMARSKJÖLD
Markings, p. 79

ON BUILDING BRIDGES

Each person is an island unto himself, in a very real sense; and he can only build bridges to other islands if he is first of all willing to be himself and permitted to be himself. . . . It is a very paradoxical thing—that to the degree that each one of us is willing to be himself, then he finds not only himself changing; but he finds that other people to whom he relates are also changing.

CARL ROGERS
On Becoming a Person, pp. 21–22

✽ ✽ ✽

AUTHENTICITY AND IDENTITY

Honesty characterizes the person and enables him to create an identity, to communicate a real presence, and to establish authentic bonds with others. The individual increasingly comes to know who he is through the stand he takes when he expresses his ideas, values, beliefs, and convictions, and through the declaration and ownership of his feelings.

CLARK MOUSTAKAS
Loneliness and Love, p. 118

✽ ✽ ✽

ON HAVING INFLUENCE

Only those who are absolutely their true selves in this world can have pervading influence.

CONFUCIUS
Lin Yutang—*The Wisdom of Confucius*, p. 124

Responsibility

THE PROBLEM

When people feel their insignificance as individual persons, they also suffer an undermining of their sense of human responsibility. Why load yourself with responsibility if what you do doesn't matter anyway, and you must be on the edge every moment ready to flee?

ROLLO MAY
Psychology and the Human Dilemma, p. 31

✳ ✳ ✳

GENUINE RESPONSIBILITY

The idea of responsibility is to be brought back from the province of specialized ethics, of an "ought" that swings free in the air, into that of lived life. Genuine responsibility exists only where there is real responding.

MARTIN BUBER
Between Man and Man, p. 16

A DEFINITION

This inseparable relation of self and world also implies *responsibility*. The term means "responding," "response to." I cannot, in other words, become a self except as I am engaged continuously in *responding* to the world of which I am a part.

ROLLO MAY
Psychology and the Human Dilemma, p. 175

* * *

BEING A DETERMINANT

Responsibility is the experience of being a determinant of what happens. Responsibility is the affirmation of one's being as the *doer* in contrast to the acceptance of the role of the *object* done-to.

J.F.T. BUGENTAL
The Search for Authenticity, p. 23

* * *

CONSEQUENCES OF YOUR INNER ACTION

The ground of what I am going to be is laid in myself, every moment, by what I do. Depending on myself in my inner posture, I bear the responsibility for my being as a result of my inner action.

KARL JASPERS
Philosophy II, p. 281

RESPONSIBILITY FOR
YOUR DECISIONS

The authentic person takes responsibility for his decisions, including full recognition of their consequences.

J.F.T. BUGENTAL
The Search for Authenticity, p. 103

* * *

RESPONSIBILITY FOR YOUR LIFE

The healthy personality becomes aware of his finitude and sees his life and what he makes of it as *his own responsibility,* not the responsibility of others.

SIDNEY JOURARD
Healthy Personality, p. 14

* * *

RESPONSIBILITY FOR
YOUR CONDITION

The doctor and the pastor ask about your health, but eternity makes *you* responsible for your condition.

SÖREN KIERKEGAARD
Purity of Heart is to Will One Thing, p. 209

FREEDOM AND RESPONSIBILITY

Man *himself* must make or have made himself into whatever, in a moral sense, whether good or evil, he is or is to become. Either condition must be an effect of his free choice; for otherwise he could not be held responsible for it and could therefore be *morally* neither good nor evil.

IMMANUEL KANT
Religion Within the Limits of Reason Alone, p. 40

✳ ✳ ✳

WHEN A SITUATION ACCOSTS ONE

I say that when a situation accosts one, then that is not the time to consult a dictionary. Rather, it is incumbent upon me to take my stand before this "new" situation, it goes without saying to take my stand before it with all that I am and that I know, and to master it to the measure of my ability, to do that which is in keeping with it, to encounter it.

MARTIN BUBER
"Reply to My Critics" (in Schilpp and Friedman, p. 693)

A GREAT CHARACTER

I call a great character one who by his actions and attitudes satisfies the claim of situations out of deep readiness to respond with his whole life, and in such a way that the sum of his actions and attitudes expresses at the same time the unity of his being in its willingness to accept responsibility.

MARTIN BUBER
Between Man and Man, p. 114

* * *

RESPONSIBILITY FOR LITTLE THINGS

In what becomes of him, a man bears the responsibility for all that he so often treats as trifles of no consequence. It is a tempting self-deception to confine one's responsible acts of will to the major, eye-catching type and everywhere else to permit oneself laxness and license. . . . In the final analysis man is in big things as he is in little ones.

KARL JASPERS
Philosophy II, p. 137

* * *

ACCOUNTABILITY FOR INACTION

A person may cause evil to others not only by his actions but by his inaction, and in either case he is justly accountable to them for the injury.

JOHN STUART MILL
On Liberty, p. 15

ON ADMITTING YOUR MISTAKES

One of the essential attributes of a good leader is enough self-confidence to be able to admit his own mistakes and know that they won't ruin him. The true test is to be able to recognize what is wrong as early as possible and then to set about rectifying the situation. I made my share of mistakes at ITT and they did not ruin me. I admitted them at General Managers Meetings, often with the expression "I guess I pushed the wrong button," and then I outlined my plan to save as much as could be saved from the situation. . . . There's nothing lost and much to be gained by admitting that you're human.

HAROLD GENEEN
Managing, p. 144

❋ ❋ ❋

CORRECTING YOUR MISTAKES

A man who has committed a mistake and doesn't correct it is committing another mistake.

CONFUCIUS
Lin Yutang — *The Wisdom of Confucius*, p. 179

❋ ❋ ❋

BEING ONE'S OWN JUDGE

A mature man is his own judge. In the end, his only form of support is being faithful to his own convictions. The advice of others may be welcome and valuable, but it does not free him from responsibility.

DAG HAMMARSKJÖLD
Kelen — *Hammarskjöld*, p. 148

Courage

WHAT IS COURAGE?

Then, Laches, suppose that we first set about determining the nature of courage, and in the second place proceed to enquire how the young men may attain this quality by the help of studies and pursuits. Tell me, if you can, what is courage.

SOCRATES
"Laches"
(in Jowett, p. 66)

✳ ✳ ✳

COURAGE AND RASHNESS

Courage is not to be confused with rashness. What masquerades as courage may turn out to be simply a bravado used to compensate for one's unconscious fear and to prove one's machismo, like the "hot" fliers in World War II. The ultimate end of such rashness is getting one's self killed, or at least one's head battered in with a policeman's billy club—both of which are scarcely productive ways of exhibiting courage.

ROLLO MAY
The Courage to Create, pp. 3–4

COWARDICE AND FEAR

By cowardice I do not mean fear. Fear is the response of the instinct of self-preservation to danger. It is only morbid, as Aristotle taught, when it is out of proportion to the degree of the danger. In invincible fear—"fear stronger than I am"—the soldier has to struggle with a flood of emotion; he is made that way. But fear even when morbid is not cowardice. That is a label we reserve for something that a man does. What passes through his mind is his own affair.

LORD MORAN
The Anatomy of Courage, p. 116

✱ ✱ ✱

THE MEANING OF COURAGE

The word *courage* comes from the same stem as the French word *coeur*, meaning "heart." Thus just as one's heart, by pumping blood to one's arms, legs, and brain enables all the other physical organs to function, so courage makes possible all the psychological virtues. Without courage other values wither away into mere facsimiles of virtue.

ROLLO MAY
The Courage to Create, p. 4

A MORAL QUALITY

Courage is a moral quality; it is not a chance gift of nature like an aptitude for games. It is a cold choice between two alternatives, the fixed resolve not to quit; an act of renunciation which must be made not once but many times by the power of the will. Courage is will power.

LORD MORAN
The Anatomy of Courage, p. 61

* * *

COURAGE AS THE FOUNDATION

Courage is not a virtue of value among other personal values like love or fidelity. It is the foundation that underlies and gives reality to all other virtues and personal values. Without courage our love pales into mere dependency. Without courage our fidelity becomes conformism.

ROLLO MAY
The Courage to Create, p. 4

BEING

A PARADOX OF COURAGE

A curious paradox characteristic of every kind of courage here confronts us. It is the seeming contradiction that *we must be fully committed, but we must also be aware at the same time that we might possibly be wrong.* This dialectic relationship between conviction and doubt is characteristic of the highest types of courage...

ROLLO MAY
The Courage to Create, pp. 12–13

✳ ✳ ✳

COURAGE AS AN ETHICAL CONCEPT

Courage as a human act, as a matter of valuation, is an ethical concept. ... The courage to be is the ethical act in which the individual affirms his or her own being in spite of those elements of existence which conflict with essential self-affirmation.

PAUL TILLICH
The Courage To Be, p. 3

✳ ✳ ✳

THE AFFIRMATION OF THE ESSENTIAL

Courage is the affirmation of one's essential nature, but it is an affirmation which has in itself the character of "in spite of." It includes the possible and, in some cases, the unavoidable sacrifices of elements which also belong to one's being but which, if not sacrificed, would prevent us from reaching our actual fulfillment.

PAUL TILLICH
The Courage To Be, pp. 4–5

THE NOBILITY OF COURAGE

In the act of courage the most essential part of our being prevails against the less essential. It is the beauty and goodness of courage that the good and the beautiful are actualized in it. Therefore it is noble.

PAUL TILLICH
The Courage To Be, p. 5

* * *

VITALITY AND COURAGE

Courage is the readiness to take upon oneself negatives, anticipated by fear, for the sake of a fuller positivity. Biological self-affirmation implies the acceptance of want, toil, insecurity, pain, possible destruction. Without this self-affirmation life could not be preserved or increased. The more vital strength a being has the more it is able to affirm itself in spite of the dangers announced by fear and anxiety.

PAUL TILLICH
The Courage To Be, p. 78

A SPECIAL KIND OF COURAGE

It takes a special kind of courage to stay in tune with your feelings when those feelings conflict and seem to work against you. It takes courage to speak the truth in many situations, especially when that truth is unpopular and may bring down the wrath of others who would rather see the world differently. And it takes courage to live fully by one's beliefs and values—to persist in actions that run the risk of failure or the risk of hostility and rejection from others.

DONALD WOLFE
"Is There Integrity in the Bottom Line?"
(in Srivastva and Associates, p. 169)

* * *

BEING IN A MINORITY

If I also, perhaps, stood before the prospect of finding myself in a minority of *one* voice, I humbly believe that I would have the courage to remain in such a hopeless minority. This is for me the only truthful position.

MAHATMA GANDHI
(in Buber, *Pointing the Way*, p. 127)

ACCEPTING SOME BLOWS

The healthier person will doubtless experience many a bruise for being and disclosing who he is, but he prefers to accept these blows rather than lose himself or sell himself (his authentic being) for short-run acceptability.

SIDNEY JOURARD
Disclosing Man to Himself, p. 47

* * *

CONFLICT AS A PART OF LIFE

Conflict is a part of life, at least as we know it. How we deal with the fact of conflict has much to do with how we express our being. . . . More authentic being will see in conflict an expected part of the human experience, a possible source of new information or deeper understanding, a challenge to creativity.

J.F.T. BUGENTAL
The Search for Authenticity, pp. 348–49

TO AVOID BLANDNESS

Unless the capacity for compassion-through-understanding is supplemented by the capacity for anger, disapproval, and indignation, the result may be a flattening of all affect, a blandness in reaction to people, an inability to be indignant, and a loss of discrimination of and taste for real capacity, skill, superiority, and excellence.

ABRAHAM MASLOW
Toward a Psychology of Being, p. 122

✳ ✳ ✳

A POSITIVE SIGN

Rebellion against dehumanizing people and experiences, against authoritarian devices and pressures, is a positive sign that a particular human being is alive.

CLARK MOUSTAKAS
Loneliness and Love, p. 129

✳ ✳ ✳

A CONCLUDING THOUGHT

To fight a bull when you are not scared is nothing. And to not fight a bull when you are scared is nothing. But to fight a bull when you are scared—that is something.

ANONYMOUS BULLFIGHTER

Epilogue

WHAT SHOULD BE DONE

Wanting to lead and believing that you can lead are only the departure points on the path to leadership. Leadership is an art, a performing art. And in the art of leadership, the artist's instrument is the self. The mastery of the art of leadership comes with the mastery of the self. Ultimately, leadership development is a process of self-development.

JAMES KOUZES and BARRY POSNER
The Leadership Challenge, p. 298

* * *

BOTH SCULPTOR AND MARBLE

In the art of living, *man is both the artist and the object of his art;* he is the sculptor *and* the marble; the physician *and* the patient. . . . While it is true that man's productiveness can create material things, works of art, and systems of thought, *by far the most important object of productiveness is man himself.*

ERICH FROMM
Man for Himself, p. 27, p. 97

* * *

THE IMPROVABILITY OF HUMAN BEINGS

There are no perfect human beings! My personal judgments are that no perfect human being is possible or even conceivable, but that human beings are *far* more improvable than most people believe.

ABRAHAM MASLOW
Motivation and Personality, p. 257

SELF-ACTUALIZATION AS A PROCESS

Self-actualization is not only an end state but also the process of actualizing one's potentialities at any time, in any amount. . . . Self-actualization is a matter of degree, of little accessions accumulated one by one.

ABRAHAM MASLOW
"Self-Actualizing and Beyond"

✻ ✻ ✻

IMPORTANCE OF THE PROCESS

The person who expresses his unique nature enjoys the getting to some place, as well as the arriving. Even when there is a goal, the entire process of pursuing or moving in its direction is important, and as much a value as the *goal* itself.

CLARK MOUSTAKAS
"Explorations in Essential Being"

✻ ✻ ✻

THE PROCESS OF BECOMING

The drama of human life can be written largely in terms of the friction engendered between earlier stages and later stages of development. Becoming is the process of incorporating earlier stages into later; or when this is impossible, of handling the conflict between early and late stages as well as one can.

GORDON ALLPORT
Becoming, p. 28

HAVING A PLAN

He who roams the oceans without map or compass has less chance of successfully completing his course than one equipped for the journey.

E. MARIAN KINGET
On Being Human, p. 227

✳ ✳ ✳

THE NEED FOR PRACTICE

But the virtues we acquire by first exercising them, as is the case with all the arts, for it is by doing what we ought to do when we have learnt the arts that we learn the arts themselves; we become e.g. builders by building and harpists by playing the harp. Similarly it is by doing just acts that we become just, by doing temperate acts that we become temperate, by doing courageous acts that we become courageous.

ARISTOTLE
The Nicomachean Ethics, p. 43

DAILY MOMENTS OF REFLECTION

We cannot do without our daily moments of profound reflection. ... I call to mind what I have done, thought, felt during the day. I ask myself wherein I have erred, wherein I have been dishonest with myself, wherein I have evaded my responsibilities, wherein I have been insincere; I also try to discern what good qualities I have displayed and seek ways in which to enhance them.

KARL JASPERS
Way to Wisdom, p. 123

✳ ✳ ✳

PERSONAL GROWTH AS A VOYAGE

Personal growth is often likened to the experience of a voyage: leaving home (one's present identity, or view of self), traveling to strange places (openness to new dimensions of experience of self and world), and a return, to enlarge home in ways that befit the "larger" person one has become.

SIDNEY JOURARD
Healthy Personality, pp. 191–92

✳ ✳ ✳

MARCH ON

Thus spoke Wisdom, and laid a hand on my burning brow, saying:
"March on. Do not tarry. To go forward is to move toward perfection. March on, and fear not the thorns or the sharp stones on Life's path."

KAHLIL GIBRAN
"The Voice of the Master" p. 79

Bibliography

Ackoff, Russell. *The Art of Problem Solving.* New York: John Wiley & Sons, 1978.

Adair, John. *Great Leaders.* Guildford, Surrey, England: The Talbot Adair Press, 1989.

Allport, Gordon. *Becoming: Basic Considerations for a Psychology of Personality.* New Haven: Yale University Press, 1955.

Anshen, Melvin. "The Management of Ideas." *Harvard Business Review,* July–August 1969.

Appley, Lawrence. *Formula for Success: A Core Concept in Management.* New York: American Management Association, 1974.

Appley, Lawrence. *Management in Action: The Art of Getting Things Done Through People.* New York: American Management Association, 1956.

Appley, Lawrence. *The Management Evolution.* New York: American Management Association, 1963.

Appley, Lawrence. *Values in Management.* New York: American Management Association, 1969.

Aristotle. *The Nicomachean Ethics.* Buffalo, New York: Prometheus Books, 1987.

Barnard, Chester. *Functions of the Executive.* Cambridge, Massachusetts: Harvard University Press, 1968.

Barnard, Chester. *Organization and Management.* Cambridge, Massachusetts: Harvard University Press, 1948.

Bass, Bernard. *Leadership and Performance Beyond Expectations.* New York: The Free Press, 1985.

Bass, Bernard. "Leadership: Good, Better, Best." *Organizational Dynamics,* American Management Association, Winter 1985.

Bellah, Robert, Richard Madsen, William Sullivan, Ann Swidler, and Steven Tipton. *Habits of the Heart: Individualism and Commitment in American Life.* Berkeley, California: University of California Press, 1985.

Bennis, Warren. *On Becoming a Leader.* Reading, Massachusetts: Addison-Wesley Publishing Company, 1989.

Bennis, Warren, and Burt Nanus. *Leaders: The Strategies for Taking Charge.* New York: HarperCollins, 1985.

Binet, Alfred and Simon, T. *The Development of Intelligence in Children.* Vineland, New Jersey: The Training School of Vineland, 1916.

Black, Algernon. "Our Quest for Faith: Is Humanism Enough?" in *The Humanist Alternative: Some Definitions of Humanism,* edited by Paul Kurtz. Buffalo: Prometheus Books, 1973.

Blake, Robert, and Jane Mouton. *The New Managerial Grid.* Houston, Texas: The Gulf Publishing Company, 1978.

Blanchard, Kenneth, and Spencer Johnson. *The One Minute Manager.* New York: William Morrow, 1982.

Block, Peter. *The Empowered Manager: Positive Political Skills at Work.* San Francisco: Jossey-Bass, 1987.

Bonner, Hubert. *On Being Mindful of Man.* New York: Houghton Mifflin Company, 1965.

Bradford, David, and Allan Cohen. *Managing for Excellence.* New York: John Wiley & Sons, 1984.

Bretall, Robert (Ed.). *A Kierkegaard Anthology.* New York: Random House (The Modern Library), 1946.

Bronowski, Jacob. *The Identity of Man.* Garden City, New York: Doubleday, 1965.

Brouwer, Paul. "The Power to See Ourselves." *Harvard Business Review,* Nov.–Dec. 1964.

Bruner, Jerome. *On Knowing: Essays for the Left Hand.* Cambridge, Massachusetts: The Belknap Press, 1962.

Buber, Martin. *A Believing Humanism: My Testament, 1902–1965.* New York: Simon and Schuster, 1967.

Buber, Martin. *Between Man and Man.* New York: Macmillan, 1955.

Buber, Martin. *Hasidism and Modern Man.* New York: Harper & Row (Harper Torchbooks), 1966.

Buber, Martin. *Israel and the World: Essays in a Time of Crisis.* New York: Schocken Books, 1963.

Buber, Martin. *On Judaism.* New York: Schocken Books, 1967.

Buber, Martin. *The Legend of the Baal-Shem.* New York: Schocken Books, 1969.

Buber, Martin. *The Origin and Meaning of Hasidism*. New York: Harper & Row (Harper Torchbooks), 1966.

Buber, Martin. *Pointing the Way*. New York: HarperCollins, 1963.

Buber, Martin. *Tales of the Hasidim* (Later Masters). New York: Schocken Books, 1948.

Buber, Martin. *Ten Rungs: Hasidic Sayings*. New York: Schocken Books, 1962.

Buber, Martin. *Two Types of Faith*. New York: Macmillan, 1951.

Buber, Martin. *The Way of Man: According to the Teaching of Hasidism*. New York: The Citadel Press, 1967.

Bugental, J.F.T. (Ed.). *Challenges of Humanistic Psychology*. New York: McGraw-Hill Book Company, 1967.

Bugental, J.F.T. *The Search for Authenticity: An Existential-Analytic Approach to Psychotherapy*. New York: Irvington Publishers, 1965.

Bullen, Christine, and John Rockart. *A Primer on Critical Success Factors*. Cambridge, Massachusetts: Sloan School of Management, 1981.

Burns, James MacGregor. *Leadership*. New York: HarperCollins, 1978.

Cadbury, Sir Adrian. "'Ethical Managers Make Their Own Rules." *Harvard Business Review*, Sept.–Oct. 1987.

Campbell, Joseph. *The Power of Myth*. New York: Doubleday, 1988.

Cleveland, Harlan. *The Knowledge Executive*. New York: E. P. Dutton, 1985.

Colbert, Bertram. "The Management Information System." *Management Services*, Middlesex, England: Institute of Management Services, Sept.–Oct. 1967.

D'Aprix, Roger. *Communicating for Productivity*. New York: HarperCollins, 1982.

Davis, Stanley. *Managing Corporate Culture*. New York: HarperCollins, 1984.

Deal, Terrence, and Allan Kennedy. *Corporate Cultures: The Rites and Rituals of Corporate Life*. Reading, Massachusetts: Addison-Wesley Publishing Company, 1982.

DePree, Max. *Leadership is an Art*. New York: Doubleday, 1989.

Dewey, John. *A Common Faith*. New Haven: Yale University Press, 1934.

Dewey, John. *How We Think*. Boston: D. C. Heath and Company, 1933.

Dowling, William (Ed.). *Effective Management and the Behavioral Sciences*. New York: AMACOM, a division of the American Management Association, 1978.

Drucker, Peter. *The Effective Executive*. New York: HarperCollins, 1967.

Drucker, Peter. *Management: Tasks, Responsibilities, Practices*. New York: HarperCollins 1973.

Drucker, Peter. *Managing for Results*. New York: HarperCollins, 1964.

Drucker, Peter. *Managing in Turbulent Times*. New York: HarperCollins, 1980.

Drucker, Peter. *The New Realities*. New York: HarperCollins, 1989.

Drucker, Peter. *The Practice of Management*. New York: HarperCollins, 1954.

Dyer, William. *Contemporary Issues in Management and Organization Development*. Reading, Massachusetts: Addison-Wesley Publishing Company, 1983.

Dyer, William. *Team Building: Issues and Alternatives*. Reading, Massachusetts: Addison-Wesley Publishing Company, 1977.

Elbing, Alvar, and Carol Elbing. *The Value Issues of Management*. New York: McGraw-Hill Book Company, 1967.

Emerson, Ralph Waldo. *Emerson's Essays*. New York: HarperCollins, 1926.

Emerson, Ralph Waldo. *Essays and Lectures*. New York: The Library of America, 1983.

Erikson, Erik. *Insight and Responsibility*. New York: W. W. Norton & Company, 1964.

Fendrock, John. "Crisis of Conscience at Quasar." *Harvard Business Review*, March–April 1968.

Feuerbach, Ludwig. *Principles of the Philosophy of the Future*. New York: The Bobbs-Merrill Company, 1966.

Follett, Mary Parker. *Freedom and Coordination*. London: Pitman, 1949.

Frankl, Viktor. *The Will to Meaning*. New York: New American Library, 1969.

Freudberg, David. *The Corporate Conscience*. New York: AMACOM, a division of The American Management Association, 1986.

Fromm, Erich. *The Art of Loving.* New York: Harper & Row, 1956.

Fromm, Erich. *Escape from Freedom.* New York: Holt, Rinehart and Winston, 1941.

Fromm, Erich. *To Have Or To Be?* New York: Harper & Row, 1976.

Fromm, Erich. *Man for Himself: An Inquiry into the Psychology of Ethics.* New York: Fawcett World Library, 1947.

Fromm, Erich. *The Revolution of Hope: Toward a Humanized Technology.* New York: Harper & Row (Harper Colophon Books), 1970.

Gardner, John. *Excellence.* New York: W. W. Norton & Company, 1984.

Gardner, John. *On Leadership.* New York: The Free Press, 1990.

Gardner, John. *Morale.* New York: W. W. Norton & Company, 1978.

Gardner, John. *No Easy Victories.* New York: HarperCollins, 1968.

Gardner, John. *Self-Renewal: The Individual and the Innovative Society.* New York: Harper & Row (Harper Colophon Books). 1965.

Gellerman, Saul. *Management by Motivation.* New York: American Management Association, 1968.

Gellerman, Saul. *Motivation and Productivity.* New York: American Management Association, 1963.

Geneen, Harold. *Managing.* New York: Doubleday & Company, 1984.

Gerth, H. H., and C. Wright Mills (Eds.). *From Max Weber: Essays in Sociology.* New York: Oxford University Press, 1958.

Gibran, Kahlil. *The Prophet.* New York: Alfred A. Knopf, 1923.

Giblan, Edward. "The Road to Managerial Wisdom — and How to Get on It." *Management Review,* American Management Association, April 1984.

Gibran, Kahlil. *A Second Treasury of Kahlil Gibran.* Secaucus, New Jersey: The Citadel Press, 1962.

Gibran, Kahlil. "The Voice of the Master." In *A Second Treasury of Kahlil Gibran.* New York: Carol Publishing Group, 1958.

Gilbreath, Robert. "The Hollow Executive." *New Management,* University of California, Spring 1987.

Guth, William, and Renato Tagiuri. "Personal Values and Corporate Strategy." *Harvard Business Review,* Sept.–Oct. 1965.

Hamilton, Edith, and Huntington Cairns (Eds.). *The Collected Dialogues of Plato.* New York: Bollingen Foundation, 1961.

Hammarskjöld, Dag. *Markings.* New York: Random House, 1966.

Hersey, Paul, and Kenneth Blanchard. *Management of Organizational Behavior.* Englewood Cliffs, N. J.: Prentice-Hall, 1977.

Hodes, Aubrey. *Martin Buber: An Intimate Portrait.* New York: The Viking Press, 1971.

Hodnett, Edward. *The Art of Problem Solving.* New York: Harper & Brothers, 1955.

Holmes, Robert. "Developing Better Management Information Systems." *Financial Executive,* July 1970.

Horton, Thomas. *"What Works for Me": 16 CEOs Talk About Their Careers and Commitments.* New York: Random House, 1986.

Huxley, Julian (Ed.). *The Humanist Frame.* New York: HarperCollins, 1961.

Iacocca, Lee. *Iacocca: An Autobiography.* New York: Bantam Books, 1984.

James, William. *Pragmatism and four essays from The Meaning of Truth.* New York: The World Publishing Company (Meridian Books), 1955.

James, William. *The Principles of Psychology I.* New York: Dover Publications, 1950.

James, William. *Some Problems in Philosophy.* New York: Greenwood Press, 1911.

James, William. *The Will to Believe and Other Essays on Popular Philosophy.* New York: Dover Publications, 1956.

Janis, Irving. *Groupthink.* Boston: Houghton Mifflin Company, 1982.

Jaspers, Karl. *The Future of Mankind.* Chicago: The University of Chicago Press, 1961.

Jaspers, Karl. *General Psychopathology.* Chicago: The University of Chicago Press, 1963.

Jaspers, Karl. *The Great Philosophers I.* New York: Harcourt Brace Jovanovich, 1962.

Jaspers, Karl. *Man in the Modern Age.* London, England: Routledge, 1957.

Jaspers, Karl. *Philosophical Faith and Revelation*. New York: HarperCollins, 1967.

Jaspers, Karl. *Philosophy* I. Chicago: The University of Chicago Press, 1969.

Jaspers, Karl. *Philosophy* II. Chicago: The University of Chicago Press, 1970.

Jaspers, Karl. *Philosophy is for Everyman*. New York: Harcourt Brace Jovanovich, 1967.

Jaspers, Karl. *Philosophy of Existence*. Philadelphia: University of Pennsylvania Press, 1971.

Jaspers, Karl. *Reason and Anti-Reason in Our Time*. New Haven: Yale University Press, 1952.

Jaspers, Karl. *Reason and Existenz*. New York: Farrar, Strauss & Giroux, 1955.

Jaspers, Karl. *Three Essays: Leonardo, Descartes, Max Weber*. New York: Harcourt Brace Jovanovich, 1964.

Jaspers, Karl. *Way to Wisdom*. New Haven: Yale University Press, 1954.

Jenkins, James, and Donald Paterson (Eds.). *Studies in Individual Differences: The Search for Intelligence*. New York: Appleton-Century-Crofts, 1961.

Josephson, Michael. Quoted in "Ethics: Looking at Its Roots," by Ezra Bowen. *Time*, May 25, 1987.

Jourard, Sidney. *Disclosing Man to Himself*. New York: Van Nostrand Reinhold Company, 1968.

Jourard, Sidney. *Healthy Personality: An Approach from the Viewpoint of Humanistic Psychology*. New York: Macmillan Publishing Company, 1974.

Jowett, B. (Ed.). *The Dialogues of Plato*. New York: Random House, 1920.

Joy, Charles R. *Albert Schweitzer: An Anthology*. Boston: Beacon Press, 1947.

Kant, Immanuel. *Critique of Pure Reason*. New York: Random House (The Modern Library), 1958.

Kant, Immanuel. *On History*. New York: The Bobbs-Merrill Company, 1963.

Kant, Immanuel. *Lectures on Ethics*. New York: Harper & Row, 1963.

Kant, Immanuel. *Religion Within the Limits of Reason Alone*. La Salle, Illinois: Open Court Publishing, 1984.

Kanter, Rosabeth Moss. *The Change Masters*. New York: Simon and Schuster, 1983.

Kanter, Rosabeth Moss. *When Giants Learn to Dance: Mastering the Challenges of Strategy, Management, and Careers in the 1990s.* New York: Simon and Schuster, 1989.

Katz, Daniel, and Robert Kahn. *The Social Psychology of Organizations.* New York: John Wiley & Sons, 1978.

Kaufmann, Walter. *Basic Writings of Nietzsche.* New York: Random House (The Modern Library), 1968.

Kelen, Emery (Ed.). *Hammarskjöld: The Political Man.* New York: Funk & Wagnalls Publishing Company, 1968.

Kelly, George. *A Theory of Personality: The Psychology of Personal Constructs.* New York: W. W. Norton & Company, 1963.

Kepner, Charles, and Benjamin Tregoe. "Developing Decision Makers." *Harvard Business Review,* Sept.–Oct.1960.

Kepner, Charles, and Benjamin Tregoe. *The Rational Manager.* New York: McGraw-Hill Book Company, 1965.

Kierkegaard, Sören. *Purity of Heart is to Will One Thing.* New York: Harper-Collins, 1956.

Kierkegaard, Sören. *The Sickness Unto Death.* (In *Fear and Trembling and The Sickness Unto Death*) Princeton, New Jersey: Princeton University Press, 1954.

Kinget, E. Marian. *On Being Human: A Systematic View.* New York: Harcourt Brace Jovanovich, 1975.

Knight, Margaret (Ed.). *Humanist Anthology.* London: Pemberton Publishing Company, 1961.

Koontz, Harold, Cyril O'Donnell, and Heinz Weihrich. *Management.* New York: McGraw-Hill Book Company, 1980.

Kouzes, James, and Barry Posner. *The Leadership Challenge.* San Francisco: Jossey-Bass, 1987.

Kurtz, Paul. *The Fullness of Life.* New York: Horizon Press, 1974.

Kurtz, Paul (Ed.). *The Humanist Alternative: Some Definitions of Humanism.* Buffalo, New York: Prometheus Books, 1973.

Landen, Delmar, and Howard Carlson. "New Strategies for Motivating Employees." In *The Failure of Success,* edited by Alfred Marrow, American Management Association, 1972.

BIBLIOGRAPHY

Levinson, Harry. "Asinine Attitudes Toward Motivation." *Harvard Business Review,* Jan.–Feb. 1973.

Levinson, Harry. "Management by Whose Objectives?" *Harvard Business Review,* July–August 1970.

Likert, Rensis. *The Human Organization: Its Management and Value.* New York: McGraw-Hill Book Company, 1967.

Likert, Rensis. *New Patterns of Management.* New York: McGraw-Hill Book Company, 1961.

Lin, Yutang (Ed.). *The Wisdom of Confucius.* New York: Random House (The Modern Library), 1938.

Lipnack, Jessica, and Jeffrey Stamps. *Networking.* Garden City, New York: Doubleday, 1982.

Lippitt, Gordon. *Organization Renewal: Achieving Viability in a Changing World.* New York: Meredith Corporation, 1969.

Livingston, Sterling. "Pygmalion in Management." *Harvard Business Review,* July–August 1969.

Machiavelli, Niccolò. *The Prince.* New York: The New American Library, 1980.

Maier, Norman. *The Appraisal Interview: Three Basic Approaches.* San Diego, California: University Associates, 1976.

Maier, Norman. *Problem-Solving Discussions and Conferences: Leadership Methods and Skills.* New York: McGraw-Hill Book Company, 1963.

Marcel, Gabriel. *The Philosophy of Existentialism.* New York: The Citadel Press, 1956.

Marrow, Alfred (Ed.). *The Failure of Success.* New York: American Management Association, 1972.

Maslow, Abraham. *Eupsychian Management.* Homewood, Illinois: Richard D. Irwin, 1965.

Maslow, Abraham. *The Farther Reaches of Human Nature.* New York: The Viking Press, 1971.

Maslow, Abraham. *Motivation and Personality.* New York: HarperCollins, 1970.

Maslow, Abraham. "Self-Actualizing and Beyond." In *Challenges of Humanistic Psychology,* edited by J.F.T. Bugental.

Maslow, Abraham. "Synanon and Eupsychia." *Journal of Humanistic Psychology*, July 1967.

Maslow, Abraham. *Toward a Psychology of Being.* New York: Van Nostrand Reinhold Company, 1968.

Maslow, Bertha (Ed.). *Abraham Maslow: A Memorial Volume.* Pacific Grove, California: Brooks/Cole Publishing Company, 1972.

May, Rollo. *The Courage to Create.* New York: W.W. Norton & Company, 1975.

May, Rollo. *Love and Will.* New York: W. W. Norton & Company, 1969.

May, Rollo. *Man's Search for Himself.* New York: W. W. Norton & Company, 1953.

May, Rollo. *Psychology and the Human Dilemma.* New York: W. W. Norton & Company, 1967.

McCall, Morgan, Michael Lombardo, and Ann Morrison. *The Lessons of Experience: How Successful Executives Develop on the Job.* Lexington, Massachusetts: Lexington Books, 1988.

McCormack, Mark. *What They Don't Teach You at Harvard Business School.* New York: Bantam Books, 1984.

McGregor, Douglas. *The Human Side of Enterprise.* New York: McGraw-Hill Book Company, 1960.

McGregor, Douglas. *The Professional Manager.* New York: McGraw-Hill Book Company, 1967.

Mill, John Stuart. *On Liberty.* New York: The Bobbs-Merrill Company, 1956.

Miller, Samuel. "The Tangle of Ethics." *Harvard Business Review*, Jan.–Feb. 1960.

Mintzberg, Henry. "The Manager's Job." *Harvard Business Review*, July–August 1975.

Mintzberg, Henry. *The Nature of Managerial Work.* Englewood Cliffs, New Jersey: Prentice-Hall, 1980.

Moran, Lord. *The Anatomy of Courage.* London: Constable, 1945.

Moustakas, Clark. "Explorations in Essential Being: *Explorations in Personal Growth.*" In *The Self*, edited by Clark Moustakas, New York: Harper & Row, 1956.

Moustakas, Clark. *Loneliness and Love.* Englewood Cliffs, New Jersey: Prentice-Hall, 1972.

Moustakas, Clark (Ed.). *The Self: Explorations in Personal Growth.* New York: Harper & Row, 1956.

Moyers, William G. *A World of Ideas.* New York: Doubleday, 1989.

Murphy, Gardner. *Human Potentialities.* New York: Basic Books, 1958.

Naisbitt, John. *Megatrends: Ten New Directions Transforming Our Lives.* New York: Warner Books, 1982.

Ohmann, O. A. "Skyhooks." *Harvard Business Review,* May–June 1955.

Owen, Robert. *A New View of Society.* New York: E. Bliss & E. White, 1825.

Pascale, Richard, and Anthony Athos. *The Art of Japanese Management: Applications for American Executives.* New York: Simon and Schuster, 1981.

Pastin, Mark. "Ethics and Excellence." *New Management,* University of California, Spring 1987.

Pastin, Mark. *The Hard Problems of Management: Gaining the Ethics Edge.* San Francisco: Jossey-Bass, 1986.

Peck, M. Scott. *The Road Less Traveled.* New York: Simon and Schuster, 1978.

Peters, Thomas, and Robert Waterman. *In Search of Excellence: Lessons from America's Best-Run Companies.* New York: HarperCollins, 1982.

Peters, Tom, and Nancy Austin. *A Passion for Excellence: The Leadership Difference.* New York: Random House, 1985.

Platt, John Rader. *The Step to Man.* New York: John Wiley & Sons, 1966.

Polanyi, Michael. *Personal Knowledge: Towards a Post-Critical Philosophy.* Chicago: University of Chicago Press, 1964.

Polanyi, Michael. *The Study of Man.* Chicago: The University of Chicago Press (Phoenix Books), 1963.

Quinn, James Brian. *Strategies for Change: Logical Incrementalism.* Homewood, Illinois: Richard D. Irwin, 1980.

Quotations from Our Presidents. Mount Vernon, New York: Peter Pauper Press, 1969.

Riesman, David. *The Lonely Crowd.* New Haven: Yale University Press, 1961.

Roethlisberger, Fritz. "The Human Equation in Employee Productivity." Speech before the Personnel Group of the National Retail Dry Goods Association, 1950.

Rogers, Carl. *On Becoming a Person.* Boston: Houghton Mifflin Company, 1961.

Rogers, Carl, and F. J. Roethlisberger. "Barriers and Gateways to Communication." *Harvard Business Review,* July–August, 1952.

Russell, Bertrand. *The Art of Philosophizing and Other Essays.* Totowa, New Jersey: Littlefield, Adams & Company, 1974.

Russell, Bertrand. *Education and the Good Life.* New York: Liveright Publishing Corporation, 1970.

Russell, Bertrand. *New Hopes for a Changing World.* New York: Simon and Schuster, 1951.

Russell, Bertrand. *Unpopular Essays.* New York: Simon and Schuster, 1950.

Sashkin, Marshall. *A Manager's Guide to Participative Management.* New York: American Management Association, 1982.

Schilpp, Paul Arthur (Ed.). *The Philosophy of Karl Jaspers.* New York: Tudor Publishing Company, 1957.

Schilpp, Paul Arthur, and Maurice Friedman (Eds.). *The Philosophy of Martin Buber.* The Library of Living Philosophers, Volume XII. La Salle, Illinois: The Open Court Publishing Co., 1967.

Schweitzer, Albert. *Albert Schweitzer: An Anthology.* Edited by Charles R. Joy. Boston: Beacon Press, 1947.

Shea, Gordon. *Building Trust in the Workplace.* New York: American Management Association, 1984.

Solomon, Robert, and Kristine Hanson. *Above the Bottom Line: An Introduction to Business Ethics.* New York: Harcourt Brace Jovanovich, 1983.

Srivastva, Suresh, and Associates. *Executive Integrity: The Search for High Human Values in Organizational Life.* San Francisco: Jossey-Bass, 1988.

Swift, Marvin. "Clear Writing Means Clear Thinking Means . . . " *Harvard Business Review,* Jan.–Feb.1973.

Tagore, Rabindranath. *Personality.* New York: Macmillan Publishing Company, 1918.

Taylor, Frederick. *Scientific Management.* Hanover, New Hampshire: Dartmouth College, 1912.

Tichy, Noel, and Ram Charan. "Speed, Simplicity, Self-Confidence: An Interview with Jack Welch." *Harvard Business Review*, Sept.–Oct., 1989.

Tillich, Paul. *Biblical Religion and the Search for Ultimate Reality.* Chicago: The University of Chicago Press (Phoenix Books), 1955.

Tillich, Paul. *The Courage To Be.* New Haven: Yale University Press, 1952.

Tillich, Paul. *Dynamics of Faith.* New York: HarperCollins, 1958.

Tillich, Paul. *The Eternal Now.* New York: Charles Scribner's Sons, 1956.

Tillich, Paul. *Morality and Beyond.* New York: HarperCollins, 1963.

Tillich, Paul. *The New Being.* New York: Charles Scribner's Sons, 1955.

Tillich, Paul. *The Shaking of the Foundations.* New York: Charles Scribner's Sons, 1948.

Tournier, Paul. *The Meaning of Persons.* New York: HarperCollins, 1957.

Tyler, Leona. *The Psychology of Human Differences.* New York: Appleton-Century-Crofts, 1956.

Urwick, Lyndall. "Scientific Principles and Organization." Institute of Management Series No. 19, American Management Association, 1938.

Weinstein, Joshua. *Buber and Humanistic Education.* New York: Philosophical Library, 1975.

Wheelis, Allen. *The Quest for Identity.* New York: W. W. Norton & Company, 1958.

Williams, Bernard. *Ethics and the Limits of Philosophy.* Cambridge, Massachusetts: Harvard University Press, 1985.

Wilson, Francis. "Human Nature and Aesthetic Growth." In *The Self,* edited by Clark Moustakas. New York: Harper & Row, 1956.

Woodworth, Robert, and Harold Schlosberg. *Experimental Psychology.* New York: Holt, Rinehart and Winston, 1938.

Zaleznik, Abraham. "The Human Dilemmas of Leadership." *Harvard Business Review,* July–August 1963.

Zaleznik, Abraham, "Managers and Leaders: Are They Different?" *Harvard Business Review,* May–June 1977.

Author Index

Subject Index